P9-DHT-322

680.92   George, Phyllis
GEO   Craft in America

13C7646

$39.95   13BT00558

DATE			
T			

D E GAVIT JR SR HIGH SCHOOL
1670 175TH STREET
HAMMOND, IN 46324

BAKER & TAYLOR BOOKS

CRAFT IN AMERICA

Celebrating the Creative Work of the Hand

Gavit School
Library Media Center

Ga...
Library Media Center

CRAFT IN AMERICA

Celebrating the Creative Work of the Hand

Phyllis George

THE SUMMIT GROUP   FORT WORTH TEXAS

THE SUMMIT GROUP

1227 WEST MAGNOLIA, SUITE 500, FORT WORTH, TEXAS 76104
© 1993 by The Summit Group. All rights reserved. This document may
not be duplicated in any way without the expressed written consent of
the publisher. Making copies of this document, or any portion of it for any
purpose other than your own, is a violation of the United States copyright
laws. All rights reserved. Published 1993.

Printed in Hong Kong.

93   10   9   8   7   6   5   4   3   2   1

LIBRARY OF CONGRESS CATALOGING IN PUBLICATION DATA

George, Phyllis.
    Craft in America : celebrating the creative work of the hand / Phyllis George.
        p. cm.
    ISBN 1-56530-081-5 : $39.95
    1. Handicraft—United States. 2. Artisans—United States.
    I. Title
    TT23.G46   1993
    680'.92'273—dc20
                                    93-32869
                                    CIP

To The Craftspeople

of America, whose lives and work
ennoble us all;

To My Children,

Lincoln and Pamela, who have
inherited my love of crafts and who will
pass along to their children
the spirit of making and enjoying
the work of the hand;

To Everyone

who believed these stories
must be told.

CONTENTS

PREFACE

Why, at a time in our history when we have machines that can make anything, are thousands of Americans making things by hand? And why are thousands of other Americans wanting to own, use and collect objects made by hand?

Although our craft movement is uniquely American, its early roots can be traced to the English Arts and Crafts Movement of the mid-nineteenth century. The movement, a revolt against industrialization, uniformly mass-produced goods and the perceived disappearance of human values, took hold in the United States in the early twentieth century.

By the 1920s, organizations were formed, professional training became available for the first time, and the studios of now-famous artists Gustave Stickley, William Morris and Louis Comfort Tiffany flourished. Unfortunately, World War I and the Depression weighed heavily on the fledgling movement, and for the next twenty years crafts all but disappeared from the American consciousness.

The craft movement as we know it today began in earnest after World War II. Two very important factors came into play in the '40s that set crafts on a course that has lasted for fifty years.

The GI Bill of Rights was enacted in 1944, providing thousands of veterans with the opportunity to earn a college education. Many of them, reacting to the horrors of war and looking for a career that embodied human values, chose to study a form of craft, wherein they found a unity of the hand and the spirit.

For the first time in history, crafts began to be taught in art departments of major colleges and universities. Craft instruction had previously been the province of the family, or the community, and excellence had been seen simply as the ability to repeat and refine a traditional technique or pattern. When craft instruction moved to the university and became part of the art department, it was inevitable that the emphasis would be placed on the creation of original work, and that students would be challenged to find new and bold solutions.

It was the combination of these two factors — large numbers of people pursuing craft as a career direction and craft being taught as a creative activity – that made American crafts unique.

Most of the people who graduated with degrees in the craft disciplines of the '40s and '50s went on to teach in a rapidly expanding educational system. It is interesting to note that prior to 1938 there were only four schools in the U.S. that offered training in craft. In 1993, 165 colleges and universities offer a degree in some type of craft education.

But even that enormous growth could not absorb all of the talented people who knew how to make beautiful things. By the mid-'60s, craft teaching jobs were almost nonexistent.

At the same time that teaching jobs waned, the alternative, drop-out lifestyle was flourishing in America. Many talented craftspeople left their urban backgrounds and moved "back to the earth," relocating in Vermont, California, the Southwest and many rural spots in between. Once there, they still needed to make a living, so they began using their skills to make ceramics, quilts, baskets, goblets, perfume bottles, furniture and jewelry. Who could ever forget the brown mug and the macrame plant-hanger of the late 1960s?

A component of the "back to the earth" movement was the development of an appreciation of handmade things. The makers quickly found an appreciative audience which was turning away from the age of molded plastic.

When the American Craft Council moved its Northeast Craft Fair to Rhinebeck, New York in 1973, crafts moved into the mainstream and thereafter became an essential part of the American art experience.

As craft fairs popped up all over the country, and galleries, specialty and department stores witnessed the public's appetite for bright, beautiful, handmade objects, they began adding them to their merchandise mix. Suddenly, craftspeople were selling to wholesale accounts all over the country, thereby ensuring their ability to make a year-round living .

Individual craftspeople and small studios are flourishing today in all fifty states. The craft movement, now sometimes referred to as an industry, claims more than three billion dollars in annual sales. But it is important to recognize that it is the people who understand and appreciate crafts who have made this revolution possible. Without an audience, this latest craft movement would have disappeared just as quickly as each of the early ones did.

People in the '90s buy crafts for a variety of reasons. Some appreciate fine craftsmanship and value the attention to detail that is rarely found in today's commercially made objects. Others find owning crafts a superb and special way to personalize their own environments and to express their particular taste. Still others find the makers themselves the appealing aspect of owning crafts. Being personally involved with a craftsperson, knowing his or her own story, enhances the value of the object. In addition, crafts are still affordable, and many craftspeople are willing and prepared to do special commissions.

As long as there is an appreciative audience that understands why handmade objects are rare and special, there will be people to create them. This book will introduce you to a few of America's greatest resources.

Carol Sedestrom Ross

INTRODUCTION

The year 1993 will always be remembered as the year America saluted its craftspeople on a national scale. The United States Congress officially proclaimed it the "Year of American Craft," and hundreds of organizations and thousands of volunteers under the YOAC banner launched a full year of exhibits, craft festivals, celebrations and special events to showcase the creative work of American hands.

It has been a gratifying experience for me to be the National Honorary Chair and spokesperson for YOAC. I am proud to be associated with this effort to preserve and perpetuate the skills, knowledge and vision of American craftspeople, whose creations become heirlooms passed down from generation to generation.

My association with art and craft began fourteen years ago when I moved to the beautiful Bluegrass State of Kentucky. As First Lady of Kentucky, I became an enthusiastic supporter and collector of crafts. I fell in love with the quilts, baskets, furniture and pottery I collected from my state, and the people who made them became my friends.

Crafts are cherished items people use, display, decorate with, and wear. They have enriched my life and I have made it one of my missions to make others aware of these treasures. Promoting craft is no longer just a hobby for me; it has become a passion.

In 1981, I worked with a dedicated group of craft enthusiasts to found the Kentucky Art and Craft Foundation. For over a decade this private, nonprofit organization has been a driving force in the promotion of Kentucky crafts nationally and internationally, and has served as a model for similar craft organizations around the country.

My book, *Kentucky Crafts: Handmade and Heartfelt*, featured the handcrafted workmanship of forty-eight Kentucky craftspeople, and was published in 1989.

I am fortunate that my career has taken me to every region of this country. No matter where I go, I find fascinating people pursuing art and craft at a very high level. Their lives and their cultures may be as different as the crafts they make, but there is a common thread which binds them all—a creative spirit that inspires them to express themselves by making beautiful things with their hands.

America's response to the craft movement as a new art form has in turn empowered these gifted artisans to continue doing what they love, and for many it has provided a way for them to make a living and support their families.

We are blessed in this country with a wide variety of artists and craftspeople—some five hundred thousand it is reported—working either full-time or part-time in their field. This book will introduce you to just a few of these fascinating people.

With the invaluable assistance of our state YOAC coordinators, we received information and stories about hundreds of craftspeople from all fifty states. Our publisher had a very difficult time deciding who to feature from all these incredibly talented people. We could literally have published volumes of books.

Our book only scratches the surface of the contemporary American craft scene, but it will introduce you to a colorful cross-section of craftspeople, representing many cultures and regions. From the mesas of Arizona to the mountains of Appalachia you will see everything from primitive folk art to the finest contemporary furniture. We have highlighted unique crafts indigenous to their regions, including works in fiber, metal, paper, wood, leather, ceramics and glass. These outstanding crafts are as diverse as the "melting pot" of people who made them, making this book a true photo-collage of American creativity.

My sincere and heartfelt thanks go out to everyone who worked tirelessly and diligently on this project. It was an enormous undertaking, but a rewarding one. I am indebted to my dear friends, Carol and Bill Butler, for helping me produce this book. I also want to thank Susie Gray, Hortense Green, Lois Moran, Rita Steinberg and Carol Sedestrom Ross for their guidance, advice and support. I am grateful to the board members of the American Craft Council and to the YOAC Executive Committee and State Coordinators for introducing me to craftspeople all over the country. I also want to thank Deborah Alexander, Lin Willard, Dee Emmerson and Hayley Hoffman for their hard work and valuable contributions to the book.

Most importantly, I wish to express my deepest respect and profound thanks to the craftspeople who shared their time and personal stories with us, and whose spirit we celebrate in this commemorative volume.

Join me now as we salute one of this country's best-kept secrets—our American craftspeople.

Phyllis George

THE SOUTH

JERRY BROWN

Potter; Hamilton, Alabama

Jerry Brown was born to pottery. Nine generations of the Brown family, including his father, Horace "Jug" Brown, have been making pots and jugs from the rich clay of Alabama for more than fifty years. "My brother and I were making small pieces back before we started first grade," Brown says.

A death in the family and equipment theft in the 1960s knocked Brown out of the pottery business for twenty years, but the pull of the family craft drew him back in the 1980s. At a time when many of the old potting families were calling it quits, Jerry Brown found both local and national customers ready for the decorative churns, face jugs, pitchers and pots that were in the Brown family repertoire. Basic supplies weren't a problem. The pit where Brown mines his clay is at least one hundred years old, and will last many more generations.

Brown might be the only potter in America still using a mule-powered clay mill. He doesn't have to, but using the mule to turn the mill is part of the old-time tradition he likes to preserve, and it gives his work a big dose of country charm. Brown likes to tell his many visitors this story about the mule:

"That mule will stop working if you leave her alone. I can't stand out there all day, so what I do is I blindfold the mule and hang a little tape recorder off her harness. The tape is me talking for a couple of hours, so the mule just goes around and around thinking I'm right there with her."

Face jugs (upper left) are a Brown family trademark, as are the butter churns (left).

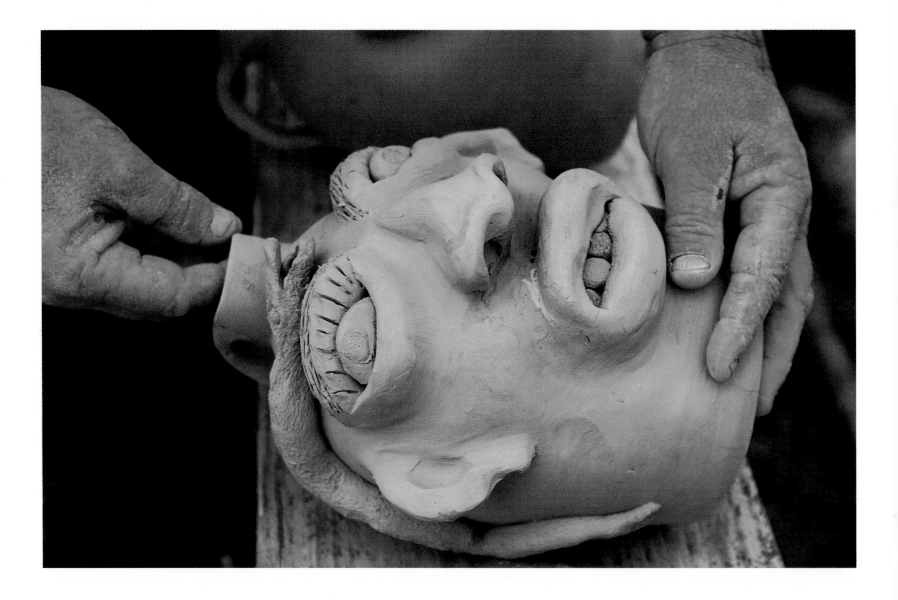

(Right) Jerry Brown sells to stores, goes to craft fairs, and takes care of some customers by mail, but he sells to many of his customers the old-fashioned way — by the side of the road.

Face jugs (left) are uniquely southern pottery forms. Since they are found all over the South, historians speculate that they might have originated with slave artisans who were mimicking African art forms. Brown's face jugs, often called "ugly jugs," continue the jug line that goes back eight generations.

A whimsical Jerry Brown cookie jar.

YVONNE WELLS

Quilter; Tuscaloosa, Alabama

For all the accolades and awards Yvonne Wells has won over the years for her quilting, she still considers herself primarily a school teacher. A sixth-grade teacher, Wells had spent over twenty years teaching in a high school in her hometown of Tuscaloosa.

Ironically, she did not come to quilting through a teacher. She is self-taught. "I didn't learn from anyone," she says, "although my mother made bed quilts and I used to watch her. I just started doing it."

Wells's colorful quilts reveal the kind of originality that comes from this kind of self-starting. She has never been overly concerned about sewing technique or the history of certain kinds of quilt designs. Everything with Wells is about artistry and design and message. "I am not a quilt historian," she asserts. "History is important, but I want to be the person who creates quilts and makes them well. For me, this is about artwork, not tradition. My work is more like paintings than true quilts."

Wells's quilt subjects fall into four distinct types—sociopolitical statements, religious messages, the "Children's Moment," and "Picture This." In doing these quilts Wells is pursuing a craft she loves. "I quilt every day because I love doing it," she says. "This is not a job. I don't follow any rules. I am my own true boss. What my head can see and my heart can feel, my hands can create. Put it all together and you get Yvonne Wells, artist."

For someone who says she "can't sew," Yvonne Wells's intricately designed quilts are beautifully constructed. She signs each quilt she makes and sews on a triangular piece of material that has become her trademark. But technique is secondary to Yvonne, whose thoughts and messages on contemporary issues are the real reason she quilts.

Her quilts are spoken of by museum curators in artistic, rather than craft, terms, and in fact have been exhibited in art museums and galleries across the country.

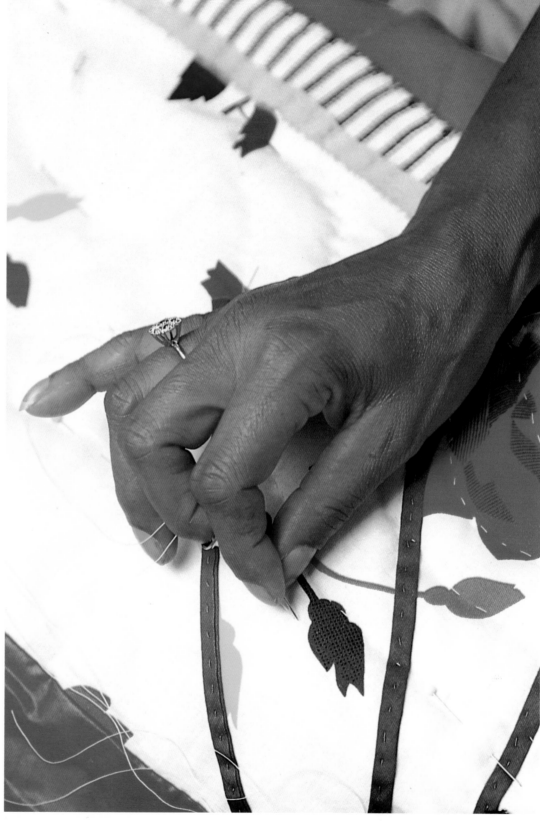

CRAIG NUTT

Woodworker; Northport, Alabama

For Craig Nutt, furniture making provides the perfect outlet for craftsmanship, woodworking technique, and humorous personal expression. His tables, chairs and decorative objects are colorful, beautifully crafted, perfectly functional and…some are shaped like vegetables.

One might be tempted to appreciate these witty constructions solely for their fun visual qualities, but a deeper, longer look will tell you more. There is a real understanding of traditional woodworking technique on display in his pieces, as well as an educated assimilation of decorative art styles. For Nutt, the work has to be both "sincere" as furniture, and visually arresting, ingenious, humorous and ironic.

Craig Nutt is one of several craft artists—instrument makers, blacksmiths, glass artists and potters—working out of the Kentuck Arts Center, a four-building complex of studios and museum space in the historic downtown district of Northport, Alabama.

Like many of them, Nutt is pursuing a personal vision, in his case using wood and the vegetable form as elements to be played with and altered. It is a unique treatment, especially in the South, where fidelity to the traditional forms is prevalent. "I enjoy breaking up the stereotype of southern craftsmen," he says. "People say, 'I can't imagine your making this and being from the south.' But it makes sense. Everybody in the south grows vegetables. They relate to the imagery.

"I personally am interested in contrasts and juxtapositions of the familiar and the unexpected, the real and the fantastic, the ancient and the space-aged, native with artifice, and the fusion of art and craft."

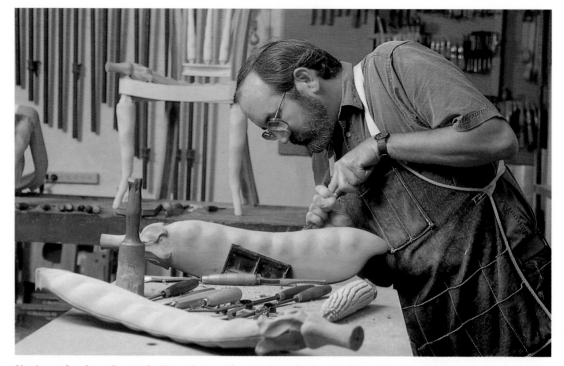

Nutt's woodworking shop in the Kentuck Arts Center is the gathering spot for tools, toys and vegetables, an unusual but necessary mix for his thematic work. The garden in front of Nutt's studio (below) provides not only food but "models" for his furniture.

At right, the "Corn Table" from the High Museum of Art Collection.

"Celery Chair with Carrots, Peppers and Snow Peas."

"White Asparagus Table with Drawers."

JOE AND TERRI BRUHIN

Potter and Weaver; Fox, Arkansas

After years of adventure travel in Europe, the Middle East, Greece, India, Nepal and other exotic destinations, Joe and Terri Bruhin and their son, Heron, put down roots in rural Stone County, Arkansas, where they turn out award-winning pottery under the name Fox Mountain Pottery.

It is a life-style they have chosen deliberately after seeing so much of the world. Their Ozark Mountain home and studio sit amid a pine forest in Red River Valley, overlooking springs, waterfalls, streams, and the full abundance of Mother Nature and her wildlife.

Joe Bruhin's pottery is known for the varied and unpredictable surface effects produced by the amazing, multi-chambered, natural draft, Noborigama-type wood-fired kiln that climbs up the side of a nearby hill. This monster kiln, handmade with over five thousand fire bricks within a metal frame, can contain up to five hundred pottery pieces within its three ascending chambers. Originally of Chinese design, the kiln requires wood fires to be placed in each of the chambers, which eventually reach 2,500 degrees Fahrenheit. In this environment, the slightly glazed and unglazed pots are subjected to a swirl of fire, ash, carbon and flying debris that creates surface streaks of orange, brown, black, tan and green. It is this random decoration that Joe Bruhin likes the best. "I just try to make a strong form and let the fire do the rest," he says.

These firings require up to fifty hours of

continuous, intensive work, so they are done no more than twice a year.

For her part, Terri Bruhin weaves on a large floor loom, usually making table linens, but she plans to start clothing designs. She also serves as a weaving craft interpreter at the Ozark Folk Center.

The Bruhins' lives revolve around nature and the pursuit of art and craft. "Living on the edge as we do," says Terri, "is definitely not for the faint of heart. We simply work hard every day, keeping our joint focus—the creation of beauty—constantly in our minds. The colors and textures of our woodland home inspire our work. Using nature's materials—clay, water, wood, fire, bones, fibers, and shells—keeps us in touch with the earth."

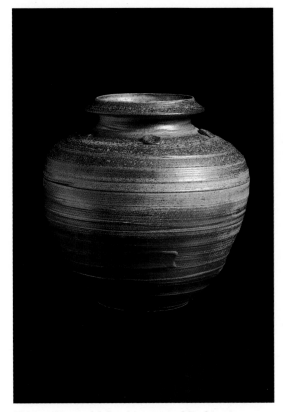

This smoky vessel (above) is a typical Bruhin piece, sturdy in form, with subtle, fire-based markings.

The unpredictable effects of wood firing are part of the joy of firing pots in the oriental, natural-draft tradition.

Gavit School
Library Media Center

The drinking vessel (left), faceted covered jar (above), and "good luck" jar (below) all reflect the carbon, ash, and flashing effects of a long sitting in the Noborigama-type kiln.

Right: Terri Bruhin's table linens are created on her large floor loom, which will soon move into Joe's old pottery studio when his new studio space is finished.

JERRY AND JUDY LOVENSTEIN

Broomsquires; Mountain View, Arkansas

For many craft artists, the integration of place, work, art and life is a seamless whole. So it is for the Lovenstein family—Jerry, Judy and son Adrian—broom makers from the heart of the Ozarks.

Theirs is a life built by hand. Their home on twenty wooded acres has been hand-built—twice—and their beautifully constructed hearth brooms, kitchen brooms, whisks and other specialty brooms are handmade, just as the pioneers made them generations ago.

It is a pioneering spirit that brought them to this land in the late 1970s, and sustained them through a period of struggling when they were learning how to market their craft. But now, with wholesale buyers and retailers placing orders for their brooms, and by winning honors and prizes at craft fairs and shows, life for the Lovensteins is a bit more comfortable. They can enjoy their daily work and their beautiful environment more fully.

Using tools from the past century, the Lovensteins re-create the traditional broom forms influenced by the Puritans and the Shakers in the eighteenth and nineteenth centuries. Jerry skillfully carves the "spirit face" on the broom handles of native sassafras, as a way to express the feeling of their Ozark experiences and inspirations. Judy embellishes the brooms with embroidered or needle-woven designs.

They say, "We use the term Folk Craft to best describe our work, for we have no academic art training. We are led by our intuition to reflect in our brooms the symbols of a homestead carved from the Ozark woods. Our handmade brooms serve as our signature among generations of broomsquires."

RUDE OSOLNIK

Woodturner; Berea, Kentucky

Rude Osolnik is considered a living master of woodturning, whose reputation in his craft approaches that of Picasso in painting or Beethoven in music. His graceful, artistic bowls, vases, candlesticks and platters are admired by several generations of woodturners, who revere him not only for his beautiful technique, but also for his thoughtful, philosophical approach to the reductive process of woodturning and the creation of art.

Osolnik has devoted most of his life to practicing and teaching the art of woodturning. Now retired from teaching at Berea College in Kentucky, he continues to conduct woodturning seminars and demonstrations all over the world.

On the crest of a mountain near Berea, Osolnik's home, barns and studio sit amid a wooded expanse of native hardwoods that serves as his life's backdrop, not for turning stock. For that he turns to the three barns and outbuildings on his property that are crammed full of stumps, fallen trees, mill rejects, deformed logs, burls, lumberyard scraps, and exotic woods such as Macassar ebony and Brazilian rosewood (often given to him as gifts). When the muse strikes, often after months or years of pondering the possibilities of a certain piece of wood, Osolnik will take it to the lathe and, using tools that he designed, fashion a bowl or vase that is usually the perfect distillation and expression of its innate form, color and design. His philosophy is simply stated: "I simply try to remove the wood in all the right places."

Woodturner Rude Osolnik has spent a lifetime learning how to "remove wood in all the right places."

REBEKKA SEIGEL

Quilter; Owenton, Kentucky

As a young girl, Rebekka Seigel noticed how good her grandmother was with needle and thread, and how many quilts were in her home. As a mother-to-be in 1973, Seigel perhaps felt a maternal urge to emulate her grandmother's quilt environment, and she began making her first quilt. Two years later, she finished it! Hardly an auspicious beginning for someone who, many years later, is considered among the finest practitioners of applique quilting in America.

Like many young quilters today, Seigel's quilt ideas are pictorial rather than pattern-traditional. As she says, "I am a quilt artist whose work is traditional in the fact that my quilts are all composed of three layers and can be used for warmth if necessary, but my ap-

Below, left: "Homage to the First Potter," 80" x 98"; below, center: "Mountain Dollmaker", 39" x 34"; below, right: "You Jerk Faced Weasel, You," 31" x 42".

"Pre-Pubescent Pool Party," 110" x 88".

proach, subject matter and imagery move them off of the bed, onto the wall, and into the realm of art.

"My intent is to call attention to the beauty and goodness that I perceive in the world around me, past and present; making childhood memories, natural history and current affairs all appropriate subject matter," she says. "Since my work is predominantly figurative, I incorporate and combine the techniques of applique, reverse applique, embroidery, batik and direct dye in many of my quilts."

Because her quilt process involves experimentation, Seigel likes to meet other quilt artists to share new ideas. She teaches quilt making, but learns a lot from others. "I was inspired to make quilts by my grandmother who taught me the basics of sewing, but my present approach is a result of teaching myself new techniques or taking workshops with other fiber artists," she says.

MINNIE AND GARLAND ADKINS

Folk Artists; Isonville, Kentucky

Minnie Adkins was "discovered" years ago, when her carved and painted animals and human figures were noticed by folk art collectors at craft fairs in Kentucky. They were selling for fifty cents apiece. Now they sell for quite a bit more, and are found in museums and galleries across the country.

Minnie and her husband, Garland, have lived in the hills of eastern Kentucky for over forty years. "I wouldn't want to live anywhere but these mountains," she says. They both grew up with mountain values and skills, the kind of skills it took to get along in that rough country—willingness to work hard, adaptability and handiness with a knife and gun. When work got scarce in the 1970s, Minnie took up her whittling knife and carved some animals like she had seen in the window of an art-and-craft shop in town. Recognition for her work came slowly, but her reputation has grown to where she is routinely included in folk art publications, and recently was given the Centre College Jane Morton Norton Award for advancing the arts in Kentucky.

Minnie and Garland are a team. He roughs out the animals from big blocks of wood or logs,

Minnie and Garland work on a new carving, clamped in a vise in the workshop of their Kentucky mountain home.

using a chain saw and a draw knife; Minnie uses a pocket knife to carve details, then she paints them.

After years of work, Minnie is at a loss to explain their success. "I'm not too talkative and I can't explain it anyway," she says. "I've just whittled and done for myself my whole life."

"Bright Blue Rooster"

Above, "The No-Count Dog"; Below, "The Three-Legged Hog."

THOMAS MANN

Jeweler and Sculptor; New Orleans, Louisiana

For those who think of New Orleans craftsmanship in terms of wrought iron and French balustrades, Thomas Mann's inventive metal constructions, sculpture and wearable art may come as something of a surprise. In design, materials and urban humor, these pieces seem far from southern in character; more German, perhaps, befitting their creator's name.

So why New Orleans? "I moved to New Orleans because of the artistic ambience of the city," says Mann. "I went there to exhibit my work at the Jazz and Heritage Festival. As a result, I fell in love with the city." At first, he came down from Pennsylvania for six months at a time. Eventually, the charm of the city pulled him in all the way.

His fascination with high-tech materials, like exotic plastics and mechanical debris from the space program, is used to great comic effect in everything from pins to sculptures. From industrial hardware and electronic scraps, us-

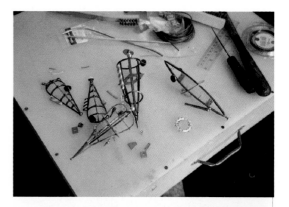

ing copper, bronze and brass, Mann creates an extraordinarily large inventory of production items—metal "collage" brooches, necklaces, earrings and wildly one-of-a-kind decorative objects that can only be categorized as mixed-media manifestations of a fantastic imagination.

Obviously, many streams feed into this river of output. One of them is a preoccupation with graphic design and composition. Mann's balanced, visually-oriented constructions reflect his major influences, including Alexander Calder, Max Ernst and Joseph Cornell, as well as his education in technical theater.

"I got out of school thinking I was going to be a set designer," Mann says. "I built big things, that was the scale I was working in. I was actually supporting myself making jewelry while I was in school."

Currently he's in the midst of constructing his first large, public artwork for a children's park, commissioned by the City of New Orleans, which he says is like a piece of his jewelry, but fabricated to a twenty by twenty by forty-five-foot scale.

"I feel as though my mission in life is to provide the raw material for imagination. I like to think I provide people with work that makes them think and makes the thinking fun."

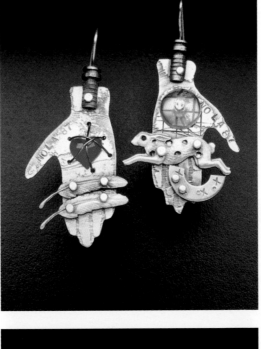

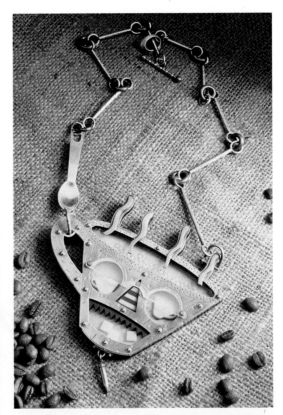

Top left: Collage Heart Earrings
Nickel, brass, glass, lucite; 1" x 2.5", 1982.

Top right: Coffee Cup Necklace
Nickel, brass, bronze, acrylic plastic, plastic laminate,
found objects; 4" x 4.75", 1991.

Bottom left: "Endangered Species—Who's Next?"
Brooch of oxidized iron, acrylic plastic, plastic
laminate, found objects; 5" x 3", 1990.

Bottom right: Snake Box Necklace
Nickel, bronze, brass, lucite, laminate plastic, found
objects; 4" diameter, 1992

MARC SAVOY

Accordion Maker; Eunice, Louisiana

Accordion maker Marc Savoy's life and art are completely involved with the music, food, language and style around his home and shop in Eunice, Louisiana—the heart of Cajun country. This seventh-generation Louisianan's words and deeds reflect a deep and lifelong love affair with the Cajun culture.

"As a young kid," he says, "I fell passionately in love with the Cajun people and what they represented. It wasn't just the music.

Other people that I met didn't have the earthiness, the power that Cajuns had."

Music was the area that interested him the most, specifically the sound and feeling of the diatonic accordion, which is distinctive to Cajun music.

After taking his old Hohner accordion apart a dozen or more times as a youth, Savoy became an expert in the construction of accordions. But simple construction of an airtight cabinet wasn't all he wanted to accomplish. He was after

perfect tone, fast response, long sustain, brilliant timbre—in short, the perfect accordion.

For legions of players around the globe, Marc Savoy's Acadian accordion is now the finest instrument of its type ever constructed. Its 532 individual parts are all handmade and lovingly assembled at a rate of about seventy finished instruments per year.

Savoy brings a craftsman's dexterity and sensitivity to the wood, but his edge isn't technical. He makes them better because he's a

After years of trial and error, Savoy has reached a level of mechanical perfection in his instruments.

player. "To convince the parts to become a musical instrument," he says, "you need to know how to play it. And 99 percent of the people who make accordions are not musicians, just craftsmen."

For Savoy and his writer/musician/ethnomusicologist wife Ann, the accordions themselves are not the whole point. Their ultimate message is in the music.

The Acadian accordion features the finest in materials, such as bird's-eye maple and Brazilian rosewood (left). Following a tradition started by his parents, Marc, along with his wife, Ann Allen Savoy, invite musicians and neighbors to their house for days and nights of music and dancing. These bals du maison have been the fountainhead for many a Cajun band, such as the Savoy-Doucet Band, whose members include Marc, Ann, and Michael Doucet, also of the band Beausoleil (right).

GEORGE BERRY

Woodcarver; Pearl, Mississippi

George Berry is a woodcarver in the true folk tradition—one born with a knife in his hand and who just naturally knows how to use one. "I started at about seven years old," Berry says. "My dad was a builder and we just always had a knife around to work with. Things just went on from there."

Throughout a life that includes many years on a Choctaw Indian reservation, and teaching and working at the Piney Woods Country Life School, Berry has carved animals with great skill and artistry. "Animals were always on the farm," he notes, "and I just carved what I saw.

"I love carving. If I couldn't sell what I make, I'd still keep doing it. I'd just keep them around, just to show them off."

SCOTT DIDLAKE

Instrument Maker; Crystal Springs, Mississippi

The task of preserving the art of making "banzas" has fallen to Mississippian Scott Didlake, formerly a computer software inventor and film producer. Banzas are the stringed-gourd precursors to banjos that black slaves brought with them from Africa to the pre-Civil War South.

It was on this instrument, Didlake asserts, that the fusion of rhythmic African music and melodic European music took place in the South, the merger from which all subsequent American music—from ragtime jazz to blues to rock—directly descended.

Eight years of experimentation and intuitive tinkering led Didlake to the kind of banza-making knowledge that must have been second nature to the African musicians who came from a very old musical tradition. Allies in the musical history field helped Didlake accumulate knowlege of the banza, but much of the original source material was visual, derived from eighteenth and early nineteenth century paintings, such as "The Old Plantation" from the Carolinas.

Banzas are made principally from gourds, which provide the sound chamber. Didlake's production process thus starts in his garden. Not just any gourd will do. Certain hard-shell strains of calabashes (some now extinct, some recovered and preserved by Didlake through selective cultivation), are the best for these instruments. To grow and cure a proper calabash takes Didlake about one year. The necks are often made of virgin heart pine, the heads are of synthetic drum material attached by brass nails, and the tuning pegs are of rosewood or ebony. When the process is over, the result is part instrument, part beautifully designed object, part living history, and part homage to the West African musicians—the "ghosts" whose contributions have been forgotten. As Didlake says, "To bring back the genesis instrument of southern music and render it in modern forms, I served nine years as an apprentice to ghosts. It is for them I have made these instruments; for their memory, for their honor, for all they endured and what they gave us in spite of it all, which is nothing less than American music in its Afro-Euro entirety. From them I learned that you don't make a banza—you grow one, and the cultivation of a fabulous calabash sound chamber is the agrarian secret to their lost musical art."

Didlake's large instruments have necks made of wenge, fingerboards of paduk, tailpieces of moradillo, bridges of Mississippi heart pine and paduk, heads of Fiberskyn II (hi-tech drum head material), real brass nails, and ebony tuning pegs. He adds banjo-style frets to many of his banzas, which the originals surely did not have.

This banza is an original design based on a fusion of elements found in illustrations of banzas from the 1820s. It has only three strings, beneficial for rhythmic playing (above).

LINDA FARVE

Basketmaker; Philadelphia, Mississippi

Native American Linda Farve produces the basket styles of her Choctaw tribe in native swampcane used by Choctaw women for countless generations. But Farve herself wasn't taught in the traditional way— by watching the older women work. She is entirely self-taught. "The elders couldn't explain it," she says. "One day I sat down and worked on a little basket. To me it was like a little puzzle. By the next day I had it figured out." With time came a mastery of that basket style, and a certain letdown. "Once I mastered it, I got less interested in it," she says. "For me the joy is in learning different types of baskets."

There is joy for Farve also in pursuits beyond the craft traditions of Choctaw women. She is active in the many issues of importance in modern Choctaw politics. Additionally, she is active in marketing Choctaw crafts, made by the traditional craftspeople of her tribe, to the outside world.

All of this can have its frustrations, too, including a shortage of basketmaking material. "Finding the cane is hard now," she says. "We don't have as much cane as we would like on the reservation, and that's a problem.

"Many of our baskets, like the double-weave cane baskets, are of tribal ancestry. The apple basket was used for wedding gifts. But nowadays our baskets are mainly decorative. People have them as collectors' items."

Southern Native Americans, including Choctaws like Linda Farve, have used swampcane and rivercane as a primary basket material since before recorded history. Their strong, durable designs were used for food, seeds, harvested crops, animals, for ceremonial and gift purposes, and as a barterable object. This highly-developed traditional skill has been passed down generationally in Native American cultures, and has survived the advent of man-made basket materials and mass production. But it may not survive the shrinking acreage of cane needed for basket-wmaking. Environmental changes might make baskets such as these a rarity, rather than an everyday, useful carrying and storage container.

AKIRA BLOUNT

Dollmaker and Fiber Artist; Bybee, Tennessee

Akira Blount might be Tennessee's most collected craftsperson. Her fabric dolls, intricate, colorful and lifelike, are found in homes, galleries and museums all over the country, and in such revered places as the Musée des Arts Decoratifs and the Musée de Poupées in France. She is among a handful of American women who have elevated the craft of dollmaking to the level of art.

In fact, an early interest in art led Blount to an art degree at the University of Wisconsin in the 1960s. But it was early motherhood that inspired the making of two dolls, which then sparked a career now spanning over twenty years.

A real love of materials, color and detail drives Blount's work. So does the idea of working in a quiet, natural place, which was the reason for the move to Tennessee from Chicago in 1979. "The connection with nature nourished my creative and intuitive spirit," she says.

Blount likes to use her wooded home as inspiration, but also as a source of material for her work. Objects she has found—such as feathers, sticks, pine cones and the like—are often used in her doll designs.

Blount's dolls are actually small sculptures, with bodies in posed positions and faces with needle-stitched expressions and personalities. This is clearly more than just stitching technique. There is an imaginative creator at work here, using fabrics, textures, props and colored pencils to achieve an artistic result.

But artistic success is not all there is for Blount. As she says, "In a difficult world, I think we all forget to stop and nurture that small child within us. We even forget sometimes that it is there. I have learned that a function of my art, besides satisfying myself and feeding the family, is that it coaxes and engages the childlike nature, and it makes people feel good! If I can affect people so they feel joy and wonder, then I have served them well."

Left: Jester carrying a violin, 27 inches high, 1989.

Above: "Pine Cone Woman,"
29 inches tall, all fabric, pine cone vest
with antique linens.

Left: "Elephant Man" (detail),
12-inch figure with mask,
lifting to reveal human face.

Opposite, top left: "Fairy Mother and Child,"
all fabric, 24 inches tall.

Opposite, bottom left: "Lion Man,"
26-inch jointed figure, all fabric.

Opposite, far right: "Moose Man,"
20-inch jointed figure with pine cone vest,
all fabric; mask lifts to reveal human face.

REN AND PAM PARZIALE

Potters; Kearneysville, West Virginia

Pam and Ren Parziale of Sycamore Pottery embody many of the classic back-to-the-land characteristics of the 1960s. They both had successful careers in advertising and design in the Washington, D.C. area, then fled the madness to re-create their lives in a less intense place where they could make beautiful objects with their hands.

But the last element of the myth—the cliché of the "starving artist"—has not come to pass for this dynamic craft couple. While things were tough at first in their new situation, the Parziales applied to their pottery works the same drive and smarts that fueled their urban careers. Twenty years later, Sycamore Pottery is a success by anyone's standards. They sell just about everything they make.

Not that material success is all the Parziales are after. They are motivated more toward custom-making their own living environment, and laboring in the service of everyday art and beauty.

The Parziales work as true collaborators. Each contributes to the output of the business. Ren designed and customized the three specialty kilns at the shop, and he oversees the firings.

Both Pam and Ren turn the stoneware bowls, vases, dinnerware and pitchers that have become their trademarks. Pam designs the products and applies her artistry to the brushwork and glazes.

"The clay is a canvas for me. I can explore

form, line, color," she says. "It is special when a particularly beautiful pot comes out of the kiln. But it's always the one you least expect, the one that hasn't been fussed over, the one that is the least self-conscious."

Ren says that, although he's been making pots for thirty years now, he can still look forward with excitement to the next day's work. "Rightness of shape is what continues to drive me and my work. Of a series of pots—let's say a dozen—some will have a rightness, others not. I think the search is why I look forward to tomorrow's work."

Both Pam and Ren have a perfectionist streak, even though they say making pots is a labor of love. The strong forms of these salt-glazed vessels (above) are a Parziale specialty, as are the brushwork and glazing of the plates (below).

THE SOUTHEAST

HARVEY SADOW

Potter; Jupiter, Florida

Perfectionist might be the word to describe ceramicist Harvey Sadow, Jupiter, Florida's renowned non-production potter, whose innovations in surface manipulations of clay vessels have had a pronounced effect on all of American pottery. How else would you describe a man whose annual output is twenty vessels, and who destroys any piece which has the audacity to be anything less than an unqualified success?

Perhaps "committed" might be a better way to describe Sadow's working dynamic. He might work on the creation of a vessel form for a week or more, but experiment on its surface for several years. He sandblasts, refires (as many as eight times), chisels and stains his surfaces to achieve a variety of unique effects. This constant testing has yielded Sadow a solid reputation as a leader in this field. His developments in dry surface coloration for raku-fired ceramics, completely experimental in the 1970s, have today become the norm for American raku.

Sadow's vessels are considered "round paintings" with his universal subject being the earth in all its visual splendor and variety. Each of his vessels is an evocation of a particular place on the earth, such as his "Chesapeake" series, his "Sacred Sites Australia" series, or the "Jupiter Diary" series, centered around south Florida. The vessels are meant to be turned when viewed, to observe a subtle progression of color.

"If you can see everything there is to see in one sitting," he says, " then I'm failing.

"My work embraces a global metaphor that weaves a story about man, earth and the whole universe, real and imagined."

"Australia, Smokey Cape," ceramic vessel, 10" x 12".

Right: "Jupiter Diary #1," ceramic vessel, 11" x 11".
Far right: "Ceramic vessel with paper."

"Jupiter Diary Series," ceramic vessel, 10" x 13".

"Jupiter Diary Series," 9" x 14", (detail).

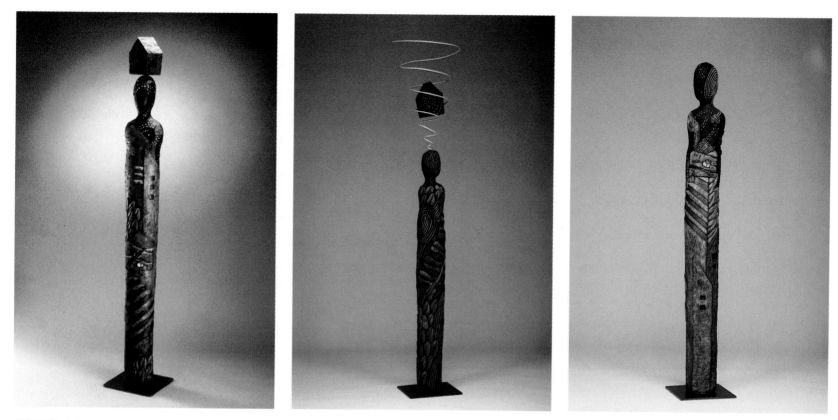

CHRISTINE FEDERIGHI

Sculptor; Miami, Florida

Symbols, and an understanding of the relationship between house symbols and human figures, are Christine Federighi's current interest. This professor of art at the University of Miami has created a series of striking works that combine representations of houses, plants and people—many of which refer to Florida and her Miami home. While allowing that personal symbols can be investigated to make them specific, she chooses to leave her works and thoughts ambiguous and enigmatic, even though it is clear that her images are influenced by Native American and aboriginal art. "Man is deeply connected to the environment and to nature," she says. "I always make that connection, consciously and unconsciously."

Many of these ceramic pieces are constructed in one piece, then carved when they are not quite hard. In the case of the stacked and multiple-attached pieces, the bottom sections are constructed first and fired, then placed on support rods or armatures.

Oil painting completes the piece, with layered coats providing a deep and varied color quality. After two weeks of drying, the piece is sealed with a clear satin polyurethane.

It is an ambitious personal vision that drives Federighi's work, but the manipulation of the medium is half the fun. "I love working the clay, shaping it, coiling it and carving it. It seems to be integrated into by life and day-to-day experience."

Above left: "Petroglyph Framework," 75" x 8" x 7", ceramic.

Above middle: "Spiral Up," 72" x 8" x 7", ceramic and metal.

Above right: "Spiral Heart," 70" x 8" x 7", ceramic.

POLLY HARRISON

Mixed Media Artist; Cedartown, Georgia

I work with trash," says environmental artist/ conservationist Polly Harrison, drawing immediate smiles from the class of fourth-graders before her. She is about to introduce them to a new way of recycling, making art out of materials that otherwise might harm the environment—such as plastic foam, cardboard tubes and boxes, old tires and newspapers and throw-away plastic lids.

Through the Georgia Arts Council's Artist-in-Education Program, Harrison helps students realize that everyone can be an artist.

"I want kids to know that we all have talent, and if we develop our talents our lives are so much richer," she says. "If we don't, it's like having a present we never open."

Harrison's own "trash treasures" have been exhibited all over America and in South America. Her art continues to transform as new "refuse" is recycled to her door.

"The consistency of my work does not lie in shape or material, but in the focus of using trash to make a statement for conservation," she says. "I've always recycled—first, because I didn't have money for legitimate supplies, then because it was an adventure finding a method for transforming the material into a work of art. Making old inner tubes look like gray velvet is easy when you weave them into expensive silk ties being discarded because they are out of style.

"A Red Cross lady pulled up in front of my studio with a trunk full of 'incompatible' computer cable from a hospital that switched to a new computer system. The city clerk saves me all her leftover dog tags, and the theater in town has a collection of my work which I traded for outdated previews of coming attractions.

"Someone once introduced me as 'an artist consumed with the desire to create.' I guess he's right. I love what I'm doing."

Conservationist and environmental artist Polly Harrison spends lots of time with students as part of her many artist-in-residence programs. Working with kids "keeps me honest about my work," she says.

Above: "Memories of Maureen," 4.5" x 8" x 8", knotless netted computer cable over electric fence wire, found objects attached. Opposite page, top left: "Princess Basket," inner tubes, silk ties and oak splits. Opposite page, bottom left: "Dog Tag Basket," mixed media. Opposite page, far right: "Earth Basket," nylon rope dyed in Georgia red clay.

BILL GORDY

Potter; Cartersville, Georgia

It wasn't unusual in the 1960s for there to be a waiting line of people outside Bill Gordy's shop on mornings when he was going to open a kiln. He was in his sixties then, and had already spent forty-four years in the pottery business. His jugs, pitchers, vases, clay baskets and the like were considered so fine that people couldn't buy them fast enough.

Gordy estimates that he has made over three-quarters of a million clay pieces in his lifetime, and despite this volume, has not had an unsold piece in the last twenty years.

Until recently, when illness finally curtailed a prolific career, Gordy had spent his life in the creation of useful, sturdy and graceful pots utilizing local Georgia clays and a variety of glazes formulated over decades of experimentation and use. His brother, D.X., also a well-known potter, and he had grown up around pottery. Five generations of the family had been potters before them, including their father, who had been a potter in the folk tradition.

Gordy is among a handful of southern potters whom historians suggest are the living links between folk potters, "art" potters and studio potters. Gordy himself is indifferent to those distinctions, concerning himself more with being a working man, making quality products and selling them at reasonable prices. He is a potter in love with his craft. "I've been making pottery professionally for sixty-five years, and I love it just as well today as when I started."

Potter Bill Gordy's skilled hands have formed sturdy vessels from Georgia clay for a lifetime.

The unusual pitcher shape in the foreground may have been originated by Bill Gordy.

These traditional shapes of pitchers and jugs are a Gordy trademark.

WATERMARK

Camden, North Carolina

Watermark Association of Artisans, Inc. is a member-owned craft cooperative, started in 1978 by thirty-five North Carolina women artists seeking a market for their work. Since that time, Watermark has grown to 740 members, and has expanded its mission to include training people to make a wide variety of crafts, enabling them to earn much-needed primary and secondary income. Watermark sells crafts created by its talented coop members at its own popular retail store in Camden, North Carolina, and has begun selling to an international market of retailers and contract buyers such as Ralph Lauren, Esprit and television marketers QVC. Watermark's craft cooperative model and internship program have been studied and praised by governments and entrepreneurial organizations around the world, which send trainees to observe the Watermark miracle in action.

Watermark has received special recognition and support from Gloria Steinem, who has arranged grants for their programs through the Ms. Foundation and media coverage saluting Watermark's contributions to women's employment and empowerment.

For many of Watermark's trainees, the craft skills they acquire mean a first job. For others, like the victims of domestic violence who are invited to participate, it can be a new beginning.

Watermark members can receive skills training in a wide variety of crafts, many of which can be done at home.

Watermark's dynamic director, Carolyn McKecuen.

CLAY BURNETTE

Basketmaker; Columbia, South Carolina

Clay Burnette practices the traditional basketmaker's philosophy of using only indigenous materials in his work. In his case, that material is long leaf pine needles, found in abundance in the nearby Carolina Sandhills. Carefully handpicking each needle from the forest bed, Burnette forms these needles into bundles, and then into baskets that are dyed in unique, colorful patterns.

At fifteen to twenty baskets per year, Burnette doesn't hurry his work. His intricately shaped and colored baskets require a great deal of time and patience, typically taking two months just to dry and dye the needles, and another six weeks to coil and sew them.

"There is a special sense of fulfillment in taking something as simple as a pine needle and turning it into an object of beauty. I can't imagine ever getting tired of doing it.

"My works are a personal exploration in color and form. Emphasis is placed on keeping things simple—simple materials (pine needles, linen), simple tools (large needle, scissors), and a simple work space (anywhere I choose to sit). From these humble beginnings, I strive to create meticulous, rhythmic forms which are spontaneous and free of tradition. I create these works for my own enjoyment with the hope that others will share the significance of their being. They are more than just baskets—they are reflections of my life."

"Overlay," dyed and painted long leaf pine needles coiled with telephone wire.

"Color Swatches," dyed and painted long leaf pine needles coiled with telephone wire.

"Rainbow Pedestal," dyed and painted long leaf pine needles coiled with telephone wire.

"Round Red Spiral," dyed and painted long leaf pine needles coiled with waxed linen and copper wire.

"Blue Basket with Beads," dyed and painted long leaf pine needles coiled with waxed linen, embellished with jet beads. All pieces are signed with a copper "CB" (initials).

ELLEN KOCHANSKY AND JAMIE DAVIS

**Quilter, Potter, Mixed Media Artists;
Pickens, South Carolina**

Quilter and fiber artist Ellen Kochansky lives in "textile heaven"—Pickens, South Carolina, which also provides her with a beautiful landscape from which to pull in visual imagery and ideas. Her one-of-a-kind fiber wall hangings and quilts have graced the walls of corporate America for many years, and her contemporary bed quilts, marketed by her EKO Quilts, have been eagerly snapped up by national retailers. Hers is a craft success story that has no end in sight.

Early in her career, Kochansky parlayed her talent for art and fashion design in a few textile pieces, which she exhibited in her small art gallery. With a 1979 grant from the South Carolina Arts Commission came the freedom to concentrate on her career, and acceptance into the prestigious Piedmont Craft Guild soon followed. From there, Kochansky built her business through craft shows, commissions from prominent art and craft collectors and, ultimately, through participation in textile shows attended by department store buyers, interior designers and home fashion retailers. This adventure into non-traditional markets has shown her what can happen when craftspeople step out of and beyond what she calls the "womb" of craft markets.

With things going so well, the only drawback is the amount of time it is taking to run the business. It is a constant struggle for Kochansky to balance her creative side with the need to manage a business enterprise.

For her husband, potter and sculptor Jamie Davis, the road to success has wound through a concentration on English literature at England's Exeter University. It was in England that Davis discovered a new calling. "I watched some potters at work one day and was fascinated, so I tried it. I did it for one afternoon a week at first, then I was doing it full-time. After working with language for so long, I found that

"Internegative," 4' x 6'.

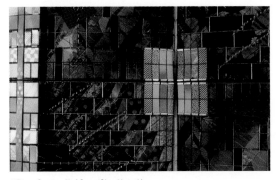

"Revolution" (detail), 4' x 4'.

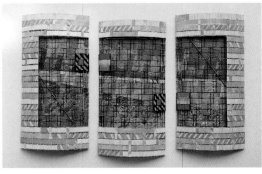

"Light Shift," 4' x 6'. Right: "Celebration," 4' x 6'.

working with visual material and my hands was a great relief."

Following the completion of his master's degree, Davis "marched resolutely through drawing, printing, stencils, figures, abstraction, etc., all in an attempt to better define my way of working."

Today, he and Ellen are collaborating on wall pieces that mix their strong visual senses with their mutual love of gardening.

BILLY HENSON

Potter; Lyman, South Carolina

I kinda like anything done the old, traditional way. It's the only way I want to do it." That's potter Billy Henson in a nutshell. Although his main business is a transmission repair shop, his heart and his family roots are in pottery, and the more old-fashioned, the better.

Henson has single-handedly revived the alkaline glaze stoneware tradition of South Carolina which flourished for generations until dying out just after World War II. "My dad had told me about the pottery business when I was younger, but I wasn't real interested in it." His involvement started with some articles in the Foxfire books featuring Georgia potter Lanier Meaders. "That's what really got me going," he says.

Before he really knew what he was doing, he was off gathering material and equipment for his first kiln. "I built my kiln from my grandfather's original kiln bricks. I set up my shop before I knew how to turn a pot. I didn't really know if I could do it or not. But I was going to get that pottery shop built, even if I was just going to look at it the rest of my life."

After a lot of reading, talking to old-timers and experimenting, Henson has reached a point where his face jugs, pitchers and vessels are prized by collectors who value the old-time styles and the forgotten methods.

"I sell everything I make," says Henson proudly, "and it sells so good because I do things the old way. That's the way most people like it. I just want to carry on the tradition."

Henson's face jugs are in the tradition of Lanier Meaders, whose story in Foxfire inspired the rebirth of a South Carolina tradition.

MARY JACKSON

Basketmaker; Charleston, South Carolina

Basketmaker Mary Jackson plays an important and dual role in basketry today. She preserves and perpetuates the low-country tradition of sweetgrass basketmaking that originated in West Africa and flourished in antebellum South Carolina, and also pursues a personal artistic vision that brings in new, invigorating forms to the craft. "I wanted to make my own special contribution to the art, so I started designing contemporary forms that had never been done in this tradition before."

This blending of the traditional with the contemporary seems just right for modern Charleston, where Jackson has her studio.

It was in the old Charleston, in slave days, that West Africans were brought to the South from the rice coast of Africa to work on rice plantations. There they modified the rice-carrying baskets they formerly had made from coiled sea grasses by using bulrushes, swamp grasses and sweetgrass. This skill was passed from generation to generation, as it still is

today. Mary Jackson learned the technique from her mother, and has taught her own daughter as she was taught. "It was always so amazing to me to see my mother make incredibly beautiful baskets from materials gathered from the wild."

As the rice culture disappeared, and the everyday usefulness of the baskets lessened, the value of the baskets increased with the skill level of the maker. That is where Mary Jackson shines. She creates original shapes with interesting handles, varies the subtle coloration of the sweetgrasses and Palmetto strips and varies the traditional sizes for a more dramatic appearance.

These stylish techniques have made her baskets distinctive, but her feet are firmly planted in low-country tradition. "The transformation of age-old shapes has emerged into a more challenging dimension, and I am now celebrating a new and calm body of work. The tech-

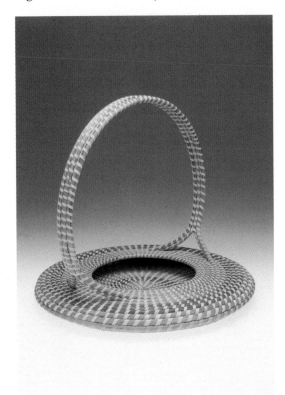

nique is the same, the material is the same as in the traditional baskets; it's just stretching the tradition to the limit of an art form."

She doesn't forget each basket's utilitarian origin, either. "Particular attention to form and function is of utmost importance because my tradition has always emphasized a beautiful basket to be used for everyday living. It is my commitment to my ancestors to work within this context."

Unifying all of Mary Jackson's basket designs is a flawless technique that admirers claim is among the best in the nation. Her forms display references to the traditional low-country baskets, but also break new ground in visual presentation.

COLORATURA

Painters of Furniture; Richmond, Virginia

Rob Womack and his wife, Catherine Roseberry, known together as Coloratura, have staked out a place in contemporary craft that might be unique. They are painters; they are surface furniture designers; and the natural combination of these interests and talents has led them to the decorative painting of period furniture.

These wildly colorful and inventive pieces are very popular with collectors, who could be attracted simply by the uniqueness and rich-ness of the designs. Others will appreciate them for the depth of research they undertake prior to painting. For Womack and Roseberry, this is not just about surface decoration. The furniture they choose to paint is chosen for design reasons; the period of the furniture is carefully researched in both furniture and art history publications; and the styles of the painting and the furniture are matched up to present a carefully-crefated statement about that era. Despite all that work, though, it's still okay to enjoy their art for art's sake.

Although they work side-by-side, Roseberry and Womack have quite different artistic voices. Roseberry "prefers to study the human figure, generally fraught with human emotions in somewhat autobiographical terms." Womack's references are more aligned with events, history, architecture and other formal artistic con-siderations. They do agree on one thing: repre-sentational paintings on three-dimensional surfaces are "tough."

"But that's part of the fun," Womack says.

Not just any piece of furniture can get the Coloratura treatment. Furniture masterpieces don't get touched. "Sometimes you have to respect the art of the original artisan," explains Womack.

But for the most part, their new ways with old furniture continue to satisfy them and their growing list of admirers. "The furniture is always different," Womack says, "and we change our style to fit the piece. That keeps us fresh."

Catherine Roseberry's "Dance to the Music of Time," enamel paint on wood.

Right: Rob Womack's "Phrenology," enamel paint on wood.

Catherine Roseberry's "No One Knows the Hour," enamel paint on wood.

Rob Womack's untitled sideboard, enamel paint on wood.

Rob Womack's untitled chest, enamel paint on wood.

Rob Womack's "March," enamel paint on wood.

Left: Catherine Roseberry's "Household Goddess," enamel paint on wood.

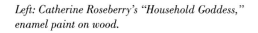

ROBERT SWAIN

Bird Carver; Hunting Creek, Virginia

The first thing I ever did, I sold. It's gone bananas ever since," Swain says. Not many artists have had the happy history of shore bird carver Robert Swain.

As often happens to craft artists, early success pulled Swain into a full-time pursuit of carving while he was managing a family garden supply business. As the cormorants, egrets, terns, ducks and herons flew and fished just outside his home on the waters of Hunting Creek, and as his finished carvings of them found their way quickly into carving collections, he decided to sell the business and make a living in wildlife art.

Swain's long-time interest had been antique decoys, and that is the look and feel he sought with his carvings from the beginning. Nothing too delicate or museum quality for Swain, who likes nothing more than for customers to pick up and handle his work. "My interest is in decoys, not actual birds," he says. "I'm creating an impression, not ultimate realism. That means my technique doesn't have to be as fine, and my painting technique doesn't have to be as perfect as the carvers who are making an exact model of a bird."

As rough as they might seem after carving, Swain takes an unusual series of steps to make them distinctly more imperfect. After carving the birds with traditional tools—hatchet, rasp, knives—Swain starts achieving a worn, aged look by alternately burning the carving and applying layers of color to it. It is a technique

originating with carver Mark McNair, but modified and extended by Swain, who has perfected the duration of the burn to achieve a unique, burnished antique look.

"I like the color of old paint," Swain says, "but obviously I can't wait around for fifty years to get the patina I want. I found a way to speed up the aging process."

Swain is happy with the "antique" niche he has carved for himself in the business, and even finds humor in his methods. "I do things to a bird carving that would send fine wood workers into shock!" he says.

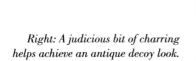

Right: A judicious bit of charring helps achieve an antique decoy look.

A cormorant.

Piping plovers are frequent visitors to the Swain dock.

A pair of skimmers prepare to take flight.

THE NORTHEAST

PETER PETROCHKO

Artist in Wood; Oxford, Connecticut

Peter Petrochko's work in wood crafts is an outgrowth of his early architectural studies at the University of Cincinnati. While studying the design aspects of that field, he became enthusiastic about making objects of wood. Over twenty-five years later, that enthusiasm sustains a full-time career as a respected producer of wood vessels and wood sculpture.

Currently he is creating pieces that range from geometrically patterned bandsawn vessels to more natural vessels that are hand carved from a single log. The use of bandsaw,

laminating, hand carving and disc sanding techniques have enabled Petrochko to accomplish vessels of varying off-round shapes. Many of these vessels are one-of-a-kind pieces that explore relationships in form, pattern, color and texture. "I am challenged by the many possibilities of what a vessel might be," he says.

His sculptural work in wood ranges from abstract carvings to organic constructions, inspired by nature or by ancient cultures such as the Incas.

Petrochko works alone, doing everything from design to final sanding and finishing and marketing. "I'm a one-man band," he says. He, like many other wood craftsmen today, is paying attention to the ecological considerations of wood work. "I am a wood nut," he says. "I use wood from all over the world. But with the exotic woods, I am using wood from sustainable sources, that have been selectively cut by indigenous people. It's my way of thinking globally and acting locally."

"Amorphic" Series, Macasar ebony, 14"h x 15"w x 20"l.

JOE HUGHES

Basketmaker; Felton, Delaware

Joe Hughes farms in rural Delaware like his father before him. You might have seen him on the "Portrait of Delaware" television show on the Turner Network in the mid-1980s. He is an articulate representative of Delaware's farming community and its heritage in folk culture. His split white oak baskets, made from trees on his farm, are shaped in traditional Delaware designs.

"Making baskets is a natural extension of my woodsman's skills," Hughes says. "I make all kinds of traditional baskets, but to me the most important thing is that the basket be strong and useful, as well as a thing of beauty. It's meant to be used, not just admired."

STANLEY JOSEPH

Coracle Boat Builder; Harborside, Maine

A small part of Stanley Joseph's busy life is taken up with the construction of a charmingly simple boat of Welsh origin called a coracle. But boatbuilding is merely one of dozens of country crafts and farming skills Joseph exhibits every day, which as a whole is an admirable experiment in living.

It all started with a book entitled *Living the Good Life*, which Joseph read and took so completely to heart in 1975 that he left his urban environment, sought out the authors and, upon finding them, bought their farm and began a re-creation of his life in their model.

Nearly twenty years later, living the simple but bountiful rural lifestyle, following the season's cycles of planting and harvesting, and mastering life-enhancing crafts like basket making, furniture making, decoy and toy carving and weaving has proven to be, indeed, the "good life."

Particularly intriguing in Joseph's long list of craft skills is the making of coracles—small round boats that once were in common use in Wales and Ireland for salmon fishing. After considerable research into the history of the boat, Joseph arrived at a solid design, fairly faithful to the original, and made of willow, which is abundant on his twenty-two-acre farm.

It is an ingeniously uncomplicated, shallow draft boat that makes a great dinghy, fishing canoe, swimming raft, or just a relaxing, floating oasis in a busy world.

That busy world must seem miles away to

Stanley Joseph, who says, "Life on the Maine Coast is hard, but it is a good life, a quality life, a way of living simply in troubled times."

Stanley Joseph studied the ancient art of coracle building, and perfected his technique by trial and error on his Maine farm. This lightweight design is a "Boyne River" type, which uses round willow shoots instead of sawn or split wood for the ribs.

To create the gunwale, Joseph weaves willow sticks around thirty-two willow ribs that have been set about every eight inches.

The willow ribs are then bent over so that the craft will take final shape.

First the sides are bent, then the fore and aft ribs.

Joseph uses heavy sailmaker's canvas to create the bottom of the boat. After stretching it tightly, Joseph sews the canvas to the gunwale.

Right: When completed, the coracle makes a seaworthy craft, perfect for short trips in relatively calm water.

LISSA HUNTER

Basketmaker; Portland, Maine

To say Lissa Hunter makes baskets is to say Rolls-Royce makes a car. Her daring, inventive, artistic, technical expressions in vessel form are the embodiments of excellence.

Her baskets exhibit a wide variety of styles, materials and techniques, and are a collection that few can match. In musical terms, she is a jazz artist, so grounded in absolute technique that only imaginative, off-the-chart solos keep her excited and engaged.

In fact, basketry doesn't commandeer her full attention anymore. Recently, gouaches, collages and wood/paper reliefs have taken some of her time. But "basketmaker" is still what she calls herself, and the medium is flexible enough to absorb whatever artistic experiment she cares to initiate.

She refers to baskets as two-dimensional surfaces, like painters' canvases, which in her case just happen to curve around a basket. But surface decoration isn't everything to her. "I love the materials," she says, "and the manipulation of those materials."

The catalog of materials Hunter uses includes paper cord, raffia, handmade paper, thread, beads, feathers, linen, leather, cane, wood, bone, rayon braid, copper wire, shells—a virtual department store of components to be mixed and matched into art. "I like having visual juxtapositions and overlays around me all the time," she says.

To explain her acuity in the visual/design arts, Lissa calls on family memories: "My mother taught me to work, my father taught me to play—two essentials of the creative life. I remember Mom playing at her work and Dad working at his play, so that the distinctions were blurred into one process of paying attention to one's life, trying to understand and enhance it. Thanks, Mom and Dad."

For the ultimate basket lover, Lissa Hunter's "Basket of Baskets," 15" x 6".

"Shoowa Homage Basket," 6 3/4" x 12".

"More Than You Know Basket," 7" x 12".

RONALD HAYES PEARSON

Metalsmith; Deer Isle, Maine

Lifelong interests in metal work, sailing and teaching brought Ron Pearson in 1971 to the perfect place—Deer Isle, Maine, near the sailing waters of Eggemoggin Reach, and home of the Haystack Mountain School of Crafts, where he is an advisor and trustee.

For a man who spent his youth around boats in Gloucester, Massachusetts, then joined the merchant marine, the pull of the ocean was irresistible. Today he and his wife, Carolyn Hecker, executive director of the Maine Crafts Association, live and work just a stone's throw from the water's edge.

Although he has worked in various metals in many sizes over his lifetime, Pearson is regarded as a master jewelry designer, elected as Fellow of the American Craft Council in 1976. His "look" is defined as elegant, fluid, classical, minimally ornamented—a triumph of simple form and design over intricacy. "Much of my work could not be any more simple than it is," he says, "but this simplicity seems to work."

A Pearson necklace or set of earrings can appear to be spun from a single piece of silver and, in many cases, they are. Of all the tools at his disposal, the most useful is a hammer which, in his gifted hands, stretches and flattens metal into graceful, organic lines and planes.

As a production jeweler, the challenge is always to expand the design inventory, and for Pearson this happens in the late winter/early spring part of the year, when there is time for

exploration and experimentation. Despite the usual, early fear that there isn't anything left that hasn't been done, a new direction always presents itself, causing Pearson to admit, "There seems to be no end to what one can achieve, and it is the challenge to explore new terrain that makes this work so exciting."

The artist in his studio, with the inviting waters and scenery of Deer Isle in sight.

Graceful organic shapes are the trademark of Ronald Hayes Pearson.

A Pearson metal sculpture rises above the shore. Although known for his jewelry, he has worked extensively in metal sculpture, in many scales.

JOYCE SCOTT

Beadworker; Mixed Media; Baltimore, Maryland

Joyce Scott, the self-styled "migrant worker for the arts," is a multi-faceted artist, performer, actor and craftsperson, whose diversified agenda is manifest in her beadwork, jewelry, sculpture, paper forms and performance artistry.

Her bead creations are part jewelry, part decorative art and part social statement. While making reference to the traditional crafts her family has produced for generations—woodwork, basketry, quilting—Scott's work is de-cidedly modern and improvisational. The tools—beads and thread—might be common, but the colorful, sculptural, message-driven objects Joyce creates are anything but.

"For me, beadwork is meditative, contemplative; a mantra for the body," she says. "It is a great time for me. I have no preset themes for the work before I start—I just start. It's like 'automatic writing'—a very free and saturated form of working.

"This work lets me illustrate all my maniacal ideas and translate all my social concerns, but it also lets me be subtle and congenial and sly about it, like a lot of artists have been throughout history."

Her social conscience and commentaries are given voice in her stunning bead creations, allowing her art to speak of racism, sexism, cultural stereotyping and politics in a highly persuasive way.

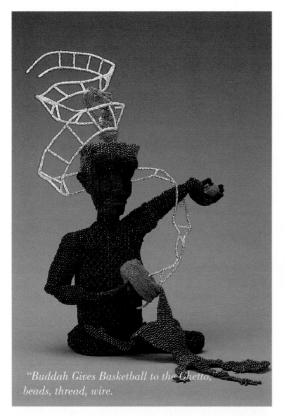

"Buddah Gives Basketball to the Ghetto,"
beads, thread, wire.

"Hunger," beads, thread, plastic, photo.

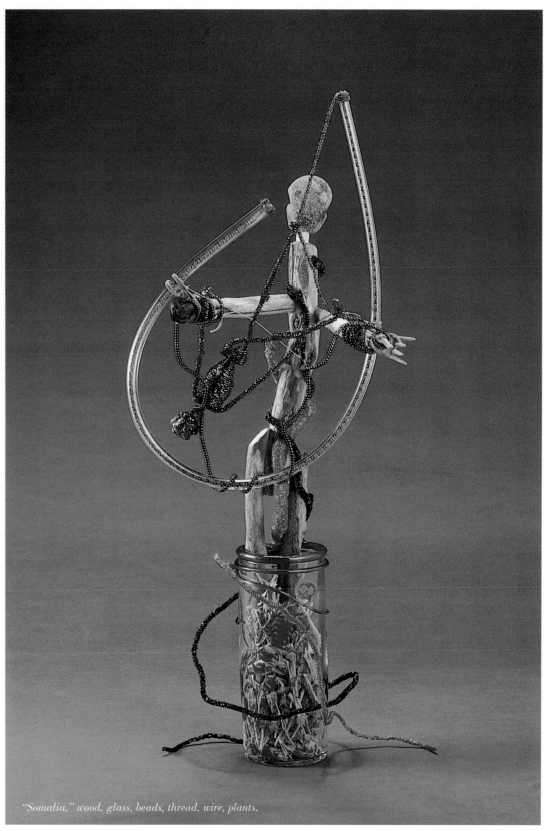

"Somalia," wood, glass, beads, thread, wire, plants.

SILAS KOPF

A beautiful view of the Berkshires beckons outside Silas Kopf's studio window.

Woodworker; Northampton, Massachusetts

To the substantial craft community living and working around Northampton, Massachusetts, Silas Kopf is affectionately known as the "Mayor of Cottage Street." The Mill Building on Cottage Street, former home to the Leeds Design workshop where Kopf taught, is now home for his woodworking studio, and the studios of many other furniture makers, potters and bookbinders.

Within this craft population and beyond, Kopf is notable for his use of marquetry techniques in his furniture pieces. Marquetry is a decorative method of joining dyed and patterned wood veneers to create pictorial images on wood surfaces. The method was first used in the west in the French renaissance of the 1700s, but has its origins in Islamic cultures.

His marquetry-decorated forms—tables, desks, clocks and cabinets—have received international recognition, including an NEA (National Endowment for the Arts) award that permitted study in France. "Originally, I had a romantic notion about crafts," Kopf says." I was going off to work in the woods. That lasted about a week and a half. As the romance wore off I found out this is a job. But the work now is nearly always interesting, and I really like the craft world and the people in it. We are kindred spirits with the same world view."

A classic, elegant chair design, with marquetry accents.

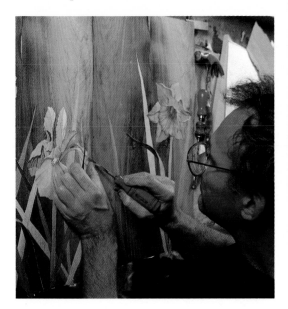

JOSH SIMPSON

Glass Artist; Shelburne, Massachusetts

Josh Simpson's work in glass is hailed as evolutionary, non-pareil, idiosyncratic, painterly.

Since his transition to glass media from ceramics in the early 1970s, Simpson has passed through the traditional and utilitarian forms—vases and goblets, a set of which resides in the permanent collection of the Corning Museum—to arrive at a place in glass where he is virtually alone. His explorations and conscious pushing of the medium into the realms of sculpture and painting have yielded unique glass objects, all of them dazzling in their complex imagery, color, shape and texture. From piece to piece one experiences millefiori, a demanding floral technique; deep new worlds of color and representational images within solid orbs of mesmerizing glass which Simpson calls "planets;" platters of glass that suggest infinite depth and complexity; and further experiments in stone-metal-glass combinations that showcase both visual industry and classic glass technique.

"Glass is a technically demanding medium," Simpson says. "It never gets boring. Even after twenty years of doing this I still have a lot to learn. There are limitless challenges. It's like being a dancer or a musician. If you really want precision, if you want the razor's edge of perfection, it requires incredible patience, and excellent physical condition and coordination. Glass blowing is a combination of ballet and weightlifting."

A Josh Simpson "planet", approximately 8 inches in diameter.

This is what Simpson means when he says glass work is like weightlifting. This physically demanding medium requires real muscle power at certain stages of the process.

The finished pieces in Simpson's repertoire, such as the Tektites shown at left, reveal different aspects of the process, those of delicacy, design and imagination.

One of the Tektite series, a meteorite glass formula exterior with an iridescent interior. Approximately 6 inches in diameter and 4 inches deep.

DONNA McGEE

Potter; Hadley, Massachusetts

Red earthenware clay is Donna McGee's medium, which she uses to create graceful but sturdy bowls, platters, pitchers, vases and teapots at her clay studio. She draws and paints these objects with scenes from the rich agricultural landscape around her—farms, dairies, gardens and the rolling foothills of the Berkshires.

Donna has shown widely throughout the United States, and has received international recognition for her work, although most of her pieces are sold regionally through shops, galleries and craft fairs.

"I love my work—feeling the wet clay, drawing, painting, contemplating, re-creating and providing pots for people who enjoy having them and using them."

Donna spends contemplative hours on her porch

The pitchers, bowls and platters make perfect surfaces for the landscapes and still lifes of Donna McGee.

Donna McGee's rural setting is often reflected in her earthenware clay. She paints colorful scenes from her immediate surroundings in the foothills of the Berkshires and the Holyoke Mountain Range.

PATRYC WIGGINS

Tapestry Weaver; Newport, New Hampshire

I want to tell my grandmother's story," says Patryc Wiggins, third-generation millworker and Aubusson tapestry weaver.

Wiggins is currently engaged in weaving a large pictorial tapestry of the town in which she grew up—Newport, New Hampshire. One of its most prominent features will be the Dorr Woolen Company textile mill, where her grandmother worked all her life, and where Wiggins herself worked before she studied tapestry.

Her purpose for initiating and developing the Mill Tapestry Project is to use traditional tapestry, as it was used in its heyday during the medieval period, as an epic, narrative, public mural that reflects to people their own traditional culture.

Milling dominates the culture in Wiggins's corner of New Hampshire, the Sugar River Valley. Newport and its neighboring villages have been mill towns since the late 1700s. Wiggins's own family emigrated from Ireland to become millworkers, and her earliest memories include the Dorr mill, three doors down from the family home.

Wiggins's nearly six-foot-by-thirteen-foot piece is scheduled to take three years to complete in its fine, twelve-thread-per-inch detail. Aubusson tapestry is a slow, labor-intensive medium, which is part of what Wiggins likes about it. The other part of what she likes has to do with the artist in the community. "I hope to expand the notions of who an artist is," Wiggins says, "where and for what reasons art is produced and for whom it serves. I am eager to share my work with those segments of the larger community who do not often find the arts relevant to their way of life.

"My project's goals are to pay tribute to the lives of area workers, including women and immigrants, and to look for the root causes of current conditions, to empower the community toward positive change for the future."

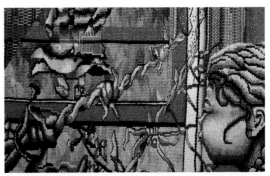

A woven sample detail.

A tapestry section detail featuring the Woolen Mill.

ALBERT GREEN

Ceramicist; Westfield, New Jersey

In June, 1988, Albert Green was inducted into the College of Fellows of the American Crafts Council in recognition of his significant contribution to contemporary craft in America. This was the latest in an ongoing series of awards granted to Green over the years.

He came to ceramics after seeing an exhibition of the work of Shoji Hamada at Rockefeller Center in 1946. This experience determined not only his choice of artistic medium, but his aesthetic as well, for the painter and the potter are one in his work. Green treats the vessel form as a canvas for rich, sensuous glazes, his brilliant sense of design, and subtle sense of color and texture.

Over the last three decades his work has been exhibited at more than thirty major museums and galleries in the United States, Canada, Switzerland, France and Japan. Of his work he says:

"For more than forty-seven years I have devoted much of my time to the study and formulation of stoneware and porcelain glazes.

"I have never ceased to marvel at the extreme sensitivity of glaze materials to kiln atmosphere and to each other when fired to the elevated temperatures necessary to bring these glazes to maturity.

"My work, like that of all high-fire potters, owes a great deal to the Chinese potters of the Sung Dynasty—960 to 1280 A.D. It was they who first discovered the means to fire pottery at these temperatures and then developed the glazes that are classic to these wares. By studying the marvelous and still technically unsurpassed Sung glazes, I learned to recognize the diversity that is possible with the relatively few materials that are able to withstand the white heat of a porcelain kiln. I also learned to appreciate glaze quality—color, texture, depth, density, reflectivity and more.

"Yet, having acknowledged this great debt, the way my pots are decorated derives almost entirely from my early interest and activity as a painter. I still ponder how best to break up the space presented by each pot in terms of dark and light, warm and cool, and all those problems faced by any painters, regardless of the ground he is using to paint on.

"For me, playing an integral part in the transformation of crushed rock and metallic oxides—the basest of materials—into the wondrous glazes that clothe the fired pot is a rich reward indeed for the effort expended."

The famous glazes of Albert Green combine with artistic vision to create masterpieces in vessel form.

Since the 1940s, when commercial glaze options were very limited, contemporary master Albert Green has developed a wide and now identifiable palette of glaze colors and textures.

If not for the vessel form, one could be observing the rich and brilliant canvas of a painter. Mr. Green studied painting at New York's Art Students League from 1936 to 1940.

LINDA MENDELSON

Fiber Artist; Yonkers, New York

Linda Mendelson has the color sense of an artist, the eye of a graphic designer, and the discernment of a poet. To channel all three of these aesthetics into a meaningful whole, she has chosen the field of fiber artistry, which allows her to use colorful wool as her palette and vocabulary.

Her highly inventive scarves, coats, capes and other apparel stretch the term "wearable art" to the limit, as these unique creations are indeed works of art in clothing form.

Where does the poetry fit in? The detailing of many of Mendelson's creations involve calligraphy, and she is apt to include a favorite passage on just about anything.

Although she treats the medium in a modern, graphic way, the craft of knitting is an ancient one, with a long social history. "It makes me feel connected to the craftsmen of the past," Mendelson says. "In an electronic age, I continue to develop the patterns and graphics for my pieces by hand."

"Walking Coat With Hearts."

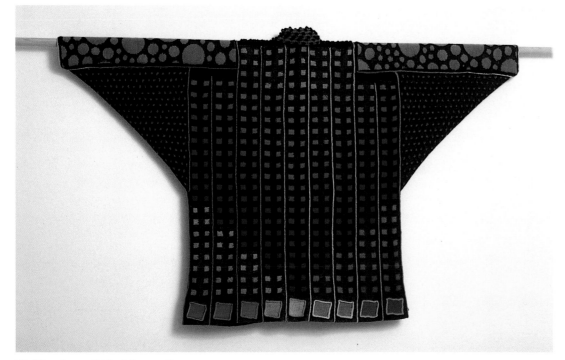

Walking Coat—"Tilted Squares."

Smock coat—"Oh What A Beautiful Morning."

"Smoke Gets in Your Eyes."

"Walking Coat With Color Progression."

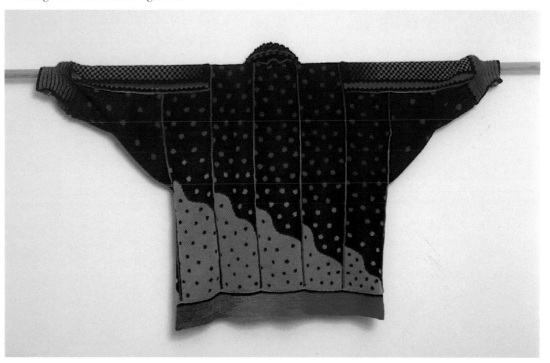

Quassia Tukufu teaches a variety of crafts to the children of New York City.

"Praise Poem."

QUASSIA TUKUFU

Multi-Media Craft Artist; New York

My father always told me to remember the three p's—'put the pencil on the paper.' Make whatever you can make when you have materials, ideas and space. There is always something new to learn and create."

Her father's words explain what has driven Quassia Tukufu to teach herself almost every art and craft there is to learn, and why she is spending her life sharing her knowledge and indomitable creative spirit with thousands of fortunate people in New York City.

Born and raised in the Big Apple, Tukufu always had a lively interest in creative experimentation. She was fascinated by the fine needlework done by her mother and aunts. Her own first exposure to crafts came from attending scout meetings with her father and aunt. "People in my family always did stuff with their hands—but never as an occupation," she says proudly.

Tukufu studied sculpture and ceramics at Temple University, then traveled and studied in Mexico and Africa. Over the twenty-two years she has been exprimenting and learning, Tukufu has taught herself quilting, basketmaking, ceramics, stitchery, jewelry-making, photography, origami, batik tye-dying, decorative botany, to name a few. Her father's daughter, there is nothing she won't try to create if given materials and space.

There is also no one she won't teach, if given the opportunity. She teaches regular craft workshops at the Brooklyn Museum, the country's seventh largest art museum, with collections representing all the major cultures of the world. Through its award-winning community outreach programs, Tukufu has inspired the creative souls of thousands of people.

She has taught ceramics to prisoners at Rykers Island. She teaches jewelry-making and other crafts to senior citizens. "They will tell me you can't teach an old dog new tricks," she says, "but I tell them I'm there to make a liar out of them."

Tukufu takes her creative road show of participating workshops to schools, community centers, group homes and hospitals. She teaches slower students to read through puppetry.

In her classes for children with cerebral palsy, teaching skills is not the focus. "We just concentrate on the experience," she explains. "Stretching, pulling, blowing—there are so many ways for the creative spirit to be expressed."

Quassia Tukufu is bottled "creative expression." Her invincible spirit permanently inspires anyone fortunate enough to come into contact with her.

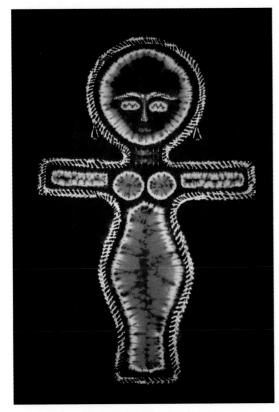

A detail from a Tukufu wall hanging.

LINDA HALE

Paper Artist; Chester Springs, Pennsylvania

Scherenschnitte is the name given to the traditional folk art of paper-cutting. Paper artist Linda Hale has immersed herself for many years in its techniques and possibilities, and now she is considered a leading practitioner of the craft.

Not content to repeat conventional designs, Hale has contemporized the art form by adding bold size and color, creating three-dimensional effects, and applying designs to unconventional surfaces, such as on folding screens and wall panels. "I've always created art with strong, graphic images," she says. "My style of paper cutting, with size, strong colors and crisp, cut edges for contrast, suits my needs just fine."

An entirely self-taught artist, Hale works alone in her studio, challenged every day by the effects paper can accomplish. "It feels good to bring individuality and contemporary style to an age-old craft. I can't imagine doing anything else."

Adding paper-cut art to folding screens brings a new and different dimension to the art form. This large screen is about 60" in height, hinged in brass and framed in custom furniture moldings.

WILLIAM LEINBACH

Weaver; Berks County, Pennsylvania

Ask Bill Leinbach why he weaves and he will reply, with a smile, "It must be in my blood."

While a student in ornamental horticulture at Delaware Valley College, Leinbach felt naturally drawn to old textiles, particularly coverlets. He admired the work of the weavers' hands, and began reading books and teaching himself the age-old art.

Ten years later, however, he learned that the Leinbach family was listed in a 1681 Prussian census as "linen weavers." Says Leinbach, "I learned for the first time that weaving is in my blood and that I had just awakened to my destiny."

Leinbach's family is extended these days. He and his wife, Edna, and two young sons live in a small village in the heart of Pennsylvania Dutch Country with seven other families. Leinbach is the village weaver; Edna makes baskets; a neighbor down the street is an old-time blacksmith who spends his free time work-

ing on their cars. It is a quiet life for these artisans and their families, and the simple yarns and fibers Leinbach weaves into his distinctive linens, blankets and coverlets reflect that lifestyle, and the beauty of an earlier time.

Bill and Edna dismantled an old log house to construct his first weaving shop, but since his coverlets and workmanship have obtained international recognition and he's been featured in major magazines—*Country Home, Early*

American Life, Weaver's—and the *New York Times*, they have had to expand the log shop to two stories. His six looms are busy these days, weaving heirlooms. Even the beds at George Washington's Headquarters at Valley Forge are dressed in some of his pieces.

Leinbach's specialty is the Pennsylvania Dutch coverlet—a handsome bed covering, traditionally handwoven as an heirloom for future generations. He weaves strong geometric patterns to create a sense of depth in the overshots of the wool yarn. His use of strong colors often eliminates the traditional off-white cotton background of the coverlet altogether, replacing it with deep wine reds, golden browns.

"My love of horticulture underlies my love of colors," Leinbach explains. "My favorites are indigo for shades of blue and madder roots for earthy reds. There is nothing more thought-provoking than the earthy aroma of a kettle full of freshly dug madder roots and experiencing the color change, as they simmer, from brownish-orange to red.

"What I do," he continues, "is a tradition. I like to think of all the skilled hands that have taught others in the past how to weave.

"A deep part of me goes into every coverlet I weave, and I pass it along to share with you—just as those old Prussian weavers shared it with me."

A completed wood portrait of Boston Red Sox great Carl Yastrzemski.

ARMAND La MONTAGNE

Wood Sculptor; North Scituate, Rhode Island

Without a trace of hyperbole, one can say that Armand La Montagne's work is as big as life itself. His job, you see, is the artful creation of famous human beings—primarily sports figures—sculpted in wood.

He is a sculptor, but he is also a trained portrait artist and an excellent craftsman.

He is without peer in his specialized niche in the art world. Visitors to the Baseball Hall of Fame in Cooperstown, New York, will see his studies of Babe Ruth and Ted Williams in the exhibition halls. Larry Bird, Carl Yastrzemski and Bobby Orr reside in the New England Sports Museum in Boston. Past La Montagne subjects also include General George S. Patton at the Patton Museum in Fort Knox, Kentucky; and President Gerald Ford at the Ford Memorial Museum in Grand Rapids, Michigan.

A multitalented artist, La Montagne begins his wooden creations by painting a life-size portrait of his subject. After that, nearly a ton of wood in a single block is reduced, stroke by stroke, to a startlingly lifelike figure, down to minute details such as skin texture.

La Montagne even goes so far as to make his own tools for nearly every job, since textural and special effects are needed for each piece. It is a laborious process, involving long hours, many months and ferocious concentration.

"In wood," La Montagne says, "you only get one shot at it, unlike clay where you can re-do mistakes. There is an inherent degree of difficulty in wood, and great discipline is required."

But despite the difficulties and solitude of the work, La Montagne enjoys it immensely. "You can't be bored with your own company," he says. "And the best thing is, with my pieces, they don't talk back." He adds quickly, "When they do, it's time to quit!"

ROBERT CRYSTAL

Potter; Shoreham, Vermont

Twenty years in the pottery business have taught Bob Crystal that handmade, high-fired stoneware has a universal and long-lasting appeal. His products are lovingly produced in a variety of glazes, all unique to his studio.

Crystal's work is often in the best "gallery" tradition, but that is not his true focus. "I make mostly functional pottery," he says. "I want people to use my mugs, pitchers and bowls in their daily lives."

It's a wonderful life (to coin a phrase) that Bob and his wife, Ann, are leading amid the beauty of Vermont. "I love working on the wheel because of its dynamic quality and spontaneity, while my wife concentrates on handbuilt work. We have no employees, as we feel more interested in the high quality and personal involvement with the work that a small studio allows."

"Our work also enables us to spend a great deal of time with our young children. Modern-day living affords most people little opportunity for such nurturing, but here in Vermont we have found a wonderful situation where studio pottery and family create an ideal lifestyle."

ELLY SIENKIEWICZ

Quilter; Washington, D.C.

Elly Sienkiewicz is a connoisseur, an educator, a writer and an expert on the Baltimore Album Quilt style of the mid-nineteenth century. She enthusiastically explores the artistic, historic and technical aspects of these quilts in her many popular books, and in lectures around the country.

In addition to her expertise, she brings people a real sense of enjoyment in the art of quilting. She is an avid quilter and quilt collector, who says, "I spend a rather terrifying portion of my quilt income on quilt expenses!"

For her, it is a small price to pay for true happiness. "For my part," she says, "the ritual of quilting has brought me peace. The world still changes, but I know my place in it more. When I study the antebellum Albums which are my love, I feel a kinship with the women who made them. What perspective on life I read in those Albums often seems still wise, and they stitched an immortal beauty into their lives as we aspire to do in ours."

THE SOUTHWEST

VERMA NEQUATEWA AND SHERIAN HONHONGVA

Jewelers; Hotevilla on Third Mesa, Hopi Reservation, Arizona

Inheritors of the legacy of Charles Loloma, sisters Verma Nequatewa and Sherian Honhongva continue the work of their late uncle, a nontraditional Hopi jeweler of international renown.

Under the name Sonwai (the women's word for "beautiful" in the Badger and Butterfly clans of the Hopi tribe, as "loloma" is the men's word for the same), these two artists have continued the tradition of their uncle, with whom they apprenticed until his death in 1991. Their choice of stones—pink and white coral, turquoise, fossilized ivory, lapis, jade, sugilite, ironwood, ebony—mirrors but does not mimic their mentor's work. The sisters were encouraged by Loloma to find their own inspiration in their jewelry designs.

Nequatewa began working with Loloma in 1970. Honhongva, her sister, joined the team a decade later. Each took years learning the jewelers' art from their mother's brother, starting with grinding and polishing stones.

"How we came to do what we do," Nequatewa explained in an interview, "rested upon his role as a master tutor. It was a gift he gave. What we managed to do with it, well, that was up to us."

What they have managed to do is infuse old traditions with their own contemporary style. It is, indeed, "sonwai."

The woman who creates the marketing magic behind the success of the nontraditional Native American jewelers featured on pages 122 through 125 is an eighty-five-year-old champion of Indian art, Lovena Ohl.

The first four letters of her name say it all. Art dealing is a labor of love for Ohl, who along with her nephew, Bill Faust, supports and represents Native American artists through her Lovena Ohl Gallery in Scottsdale and the Lovena Ohl Foundation.

Ohl has been dealing Native American art

Gallery owner Lovena Ohl with Verma, Sherian and James Little.

and crafts for forty years, ever since she moved to Phoenix to provide her asthmatic nephew a climate change. She eventually became a respected Native American arts buyer for the prestigious Heard Museum's gift shop.

To converse with Ohl is to learn that she's both knowledgeable and caring, but rumor in the buying community has it that she can also be a tough cookie when it comes to negotiating for her artists' welfare. She uses some of the income from her gallery to award cash grants through the Lovena Ohl Foundation, allowing Indian artists to enhance their talents through travel or study. A Pulitzer Prize-winning Indian author, N. Scott Momaday, praised her for "her knowledge, her discriminating taste, her appreciation of indigenous art forms and her singular dedication to the efforts of native artists."

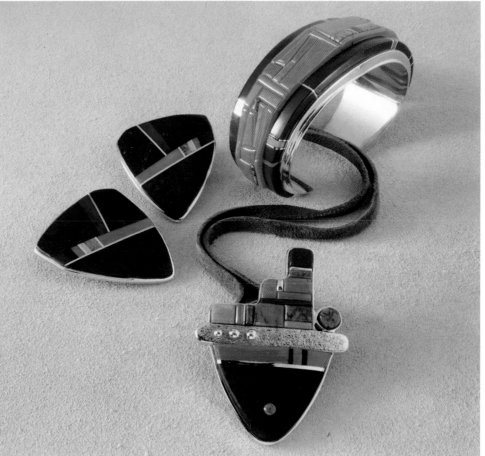

JAMES LITTLE

Jeweler, Scottsdale, Arizona

The world where James Little grew up, a land of bright mountains and wide valleys occasionally shaded by the passing of a cloud, was a silent world.

As a child, Navajo jeweler Little could not hear. Operations in his youth and again in his late teens did almost nothing to alleviate his deafness. Only later, in his twenties, could his hearing be corrected enough for Little to go to school and learn English. So it's surprising how well he speaks the language today.

"I didn't grow up speaking English," he says. "I didn't grow up in the city. I grew up on the reservation with my mother and father. They told me a lot of stories. A lot of ceremonial things, they explain what they mean.

"Because my mother weaves Navajo rugs, she showed me the designs, then I started thinking about it. I decided to make the jewelry like the rug designs."

Today James Little's unique Navajo bracelets, necklaces, earrings and chokers set new standards for Native American contemporary jewelry design. He makes everything himself, he says, without assistants, because he likes to finish the pieces his own way, "really good inside and out."

Little's brother, a painter, originally connected him with a reservation arts and crafts program, then an adult education program at Many Farms Community College. Little learned the basics of jewelry-making, then worked in the back room of a jewelry manufacturer that hired the handicapped in Flagstaff.

"They found a job for me at Flagstaff, making my own designs. When I went to school, I did my own designs, so then that's what I call my 'twisted wire' at Flagstaff," he recalls. "Nobody's seen that before. It got really popular at Flagstaff. The other jewelers, they looked at that, and they copied that," he says.

It was obvious also to dealers in the Native American fine arts community that Little showed special talent. California dealers, the Don Kirkhuffs, sponsored Little going off on his own to make original, museum-quality work.

Lovena Ohl's gallery in Scottsdale took a special interest in Little, sponsoring one-on-one language tutoring through the Lovena Ohl Foundation. He has since won regional and national awards, and his work has become internationally known. "Now I don't have any time to do something for myself," he laments. His eyesight isn't as good as it used to be, and too many custom orders to repeat pieces means he can't make as many original pieces. "But I'm still making ideas," he says. "That's no problem."

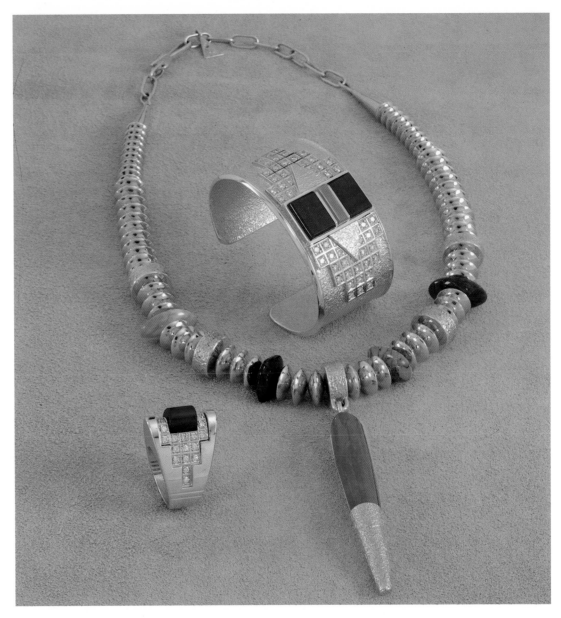

CHESLEY GOSEYUN WILSON

Instrument Maker; Tucson, Arizona

Chesley Wilson is a keeper of the sacred songs and dances of his Apache tribe, as well as one of the only makers of the Apache violin.

A great-grandson of chiefs, Wilson is a Korean War veteran who worked at professional silversmithing for twenty-five years before he gave up that career for his present one.

Although he's been dubbed an Arizona Living Treasure and a National Heritage Fellow for the instrument-making knowledge he now imparts to young Apaches, violinmaking doesn't pay the bills, so he also serves as a part-time Pinkerton guard in Tucson.

His true calling, he believes, demands that he pass on the techniques he uses to make traditional instruments: the violin (called "wood that sings" in Wilson's native language), tsisol flute and Apache water drum.

The violins are fashioned of dried agave flower stalk, hollowed out, peeled, pierced with sound holes and decorated with paint and feathers, using Apache designs including hummingbirds and wind spirits—a crescent shape.

Wilson learned the techniques of instrument-making from his uncles, Albert Goseyun and Amos Gustina.

Wilson has become an expert on the mountain-spirit ceremonies. He and wife Ruth perform Apache songs and dances at tribal gatherings, and they demonstrate the use and meaning of the violin to Indians and non-Indians alike.

"All of my life I have wanted to teach young Apaches the traditional crafts and songs I learned from my family, so the knowledge will not be lost," he says. "As the last in a string of violin makers, I am doing all I can to keep this Apache tradition alive. I hope to keep on doing it as long as I'm here on this Earth."

Chesley and Ruth Wilson with violins and Ga'an carvings.

Right: An Apache violin.

Below, "Hank and Marie." Left, "Cowabunga."

WENDY MARUYAMA

Furniture Designer; San Diego, California

Rebellious design and traditional crafts-manship merge in the furnishings of Wendy Maruyama. This San Diegoan makes furniture hip. Her fine workmanship and free-spirited ideas combine in such works as her 1992 "Cabinet for the Curious" and "A Lesson in Excess from Louis XIV."

Her hot mix of colors reveals a playful, surf's-up style of excitement about her art form, as well as the sensibility of an artisan willing to take risks. She raises the level of discourse in an art form dominated by centuries-old tradi-tion. And the furniture world listens, because she has well-grounded ideas about joinery, form and functionality. "Function is first," she has said.

Maruyama has come full circle. Raised in the San Diego suburb of Chula Vista in a traditional Japanese-American family, Maruyama entered San Diego State and took the unconventional course, studying furniture design instead of her safe route—jewelry making.

These days she teaches her furniture design to SDSU students, encouraging them to think for themselves. "Woodworking students," she says, "tend to be completely technical—mate-rials, equipment, tools—but I want them to get a sense of who they are, what they respond to, what their voice is at the same time."

Her own voice is exceptionally gifted, but she wonders whether her naiveté has been lost as she has become more technically endowed. "Sometimes the more you know," she confides, "the more restricted you are."

"Red Chest."

"Red Chest" (opened).

"Patterned Credenza."

"Black and White Blanket Chest."

"Ooohh-La-La Vanity."

"Cabinet For the Curious."

"Box on Stand."

"A Lesson in Excess."

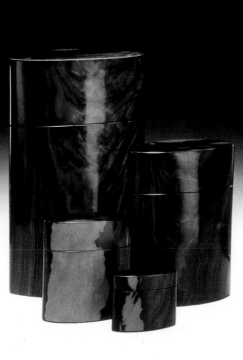

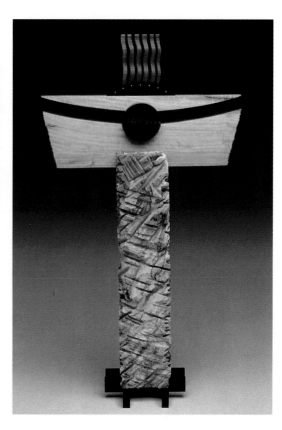

JEFFREY AND KATRINA SEATON

Wood Designer; Santa Barbara, California

Jeffrey Seaton, without thinking, calls his business a two-man shop, then corrects himself to say "two-person."

The second "man" at the shop, is his wife, Katrina. Together they design one-of-a-kind boxes of rare wood, leather, raffia, silver and copper.

The wood is sawn, constructed and sanded by Jeffrey, with leather- and rafia-application by Katrina, who splits and weaves the raffia fibers, inlaying them into channels shaped into the wood by her husband.

"I think one of the main benefits of having a husband-wife team work together is in the design aspects. Frequently, as we travel, we bounce ideas back and forth," says Seaton, who began making fine-finish boxes twenty years ago. Katrina joined him in the business a decade later.

It's Seaton's belief that a "hidden space within" subconsciously attracts people. At shows, he reports, some people will pick up every single box on display, and open each lid to look inside. "We're curious by nature—if you put a lid on something, you want to lift it," he laughs. "Anything that's a puzzle or a box that has something further than the surface, we're curious. Also it feels good to the touch—it's warm and glassy."

Seaton says he, too, was drawn to the work partly by the tactile pleasure of wood. The Seatons sand their boxes creamy smooth, with seven different grits of sandpaper. "I'm removing scratches from each grit, allowing you to see into the wood," he says. "Very few woodworkers sand it that far."

Katrina does much of the buffing and polishing, using only oil and wax to bring out the three-dimensional, light-to-dark grain (a quality called chytoyance) in the highly figured, exotic and rare hardwoods they favor.

Their latest favorite is snakewood, "which looks just like it sounds—a nice, mottled pattern like a snake's back—from Surinam, a small tree way up the river. It comes down the river in canoes."

Like many woodworkers, the Seatons have joined the Woodworkers Alliance for Rainforest Protection. "More and more frequently, I'm looking for alternative wood sources giving value back to indigenous wood growers," he says, "companies that seek legitimate, controlled, renewable resources."

SAM MALOOF

Woodworker; Alta Loma, California

The list of awards honoring Sam Maloof, master craftsman, go back decades.

He began woodworking in 1948 at the age of thirty-two and, as he puts it in his book, *Sam Maloof*, devoted to his superlative furniture making: "From the day I started I have been able to make my living working for myself and doing what I like to do: work in wood. I love the feel, the character of wood, no matter what the species, and I enjoy making objects that are both functional and beautiful."

His words—simple, straightforward, inspiring, useful—resemble his work, which is meant to be used. When the Museum of Fine Arts in Boston displayed his furniture, it was with a sign that read: "Please be seated."

Maloof thinks a woodworker who plans to design his own must appreciate all arts, and he cannot recall a time when he did not draw. But woodworking was an early enthusiasm. "I made a paddle when I was eleven," he writes, "for taking bread out of the oven. Someone once pointed out that it was constructed on surprisingly sophisticated lines for an eleven-year-old: it had a dado joint and was so well built it is still used by my sisters. It seems wood always has held an attraction for me."

Maloof completes seventy-five new pieces a year, with two assistants who shape, sand and finish the chairs, tables, credenzas and cabinets that he cuts and assembles himself. Each piece is slightly different, bespeaking Maloof's belief that wood lives, even after it has been cut. He signs, dates and numbers each of his pieces, the majority of which are worked in black walnut, a wood he prefers for its warmth, texture and workability.

Maloof's story is one of gradual, consistent success and slow, steady growth of immense respect from other craftsmen and all who appreciate refined artistry. But he has said that had he sought only material security, he would never have chosen woodworking as a career.

Self-taught in the pure sense, he remains open to the way woodworking shapes and molds him as an artist.

"I hope that I never reach the top of the mountain," he writes, "for then I must come down. Each day I learn something new."

Above: Work in progress at Sam Maloof's shop. Below: A conference room full of Maloof chairs and table.

RUBEL JARAMILLO

Santero; Antonito, Colorado

Wooden images of saints and divine persons of the Catholic Church, called *santos* in Hispanic cultures, have been part of the folk art heritage of Hispanic people for hundreds of years. These carvings, usually unpainted, are religious icons that communicate devotion to the church and its saints, and are often used in religious processions.

In the past, a *santero*, or carver of *santos*, was usually a carpenter by trade who created religious objects as a devotional act. Today, very few of these *santeros* are left. Rubel Jaramillo is one of them.

Now in his sixties, Jaramillo comes from a family of *santos* carvers over five generations. His grandfather urged him to make things with his hands, to leave behind something of himself in his work, and to preserve the family heritage.

Jaramillo's destiny, however, was a military career, beginning at age sixteen, and lasting for thirty years.

His grandfather's words apparently struck home only after his tours of duty were over, when he returned home to America from Vietnam, wounded, addicted to Valium, and disillusioned by his life in uniform. "Here I was, a war hero," he says. " But I was stripped of my glory. I had nothing left but what my grandfather left me—some carving tools and the skills to use them."

He turned to *santos* carving as a means of redirection and recovery in his life. Encouraging reactions to his work at fairs and folk festivals started him on a new career, one which now includes carving jewelry boxes and making furniture.

But the *santos* are still special for Jaramillo. He gives away most of his carvings to priests, nuns and small churches, preferring to respect them that way rather than sell them in less than dignified surroundings. He is also teaching the art to younger men, hoping to leave his legacy not only in his work, but also in the skills of those he teaches. "It's our art form," he says. "It was born here. It's ours. We will lose it unless we continue it. It's not *who* does it, but that it continues that matters."

EPPIE ARCHULETA

Weaver; Alamosa, Colorado

For four centuries, the descendents of Hispanic peoples have lived and worked in what is now the American Southwest. In her northern New Mexico birthplace, a child named Eppie Archuleta inherited a multi-generational legacy of native weavers.

She was taught to weave at the age of six by her mother—Agueda Martinez, a renowned master of the weaver's art—using her grandfather's handmade treadle loom. Today, Archuleta is herself the master weaver, the one who has passed on her family craft to her eight children, every one of whom spin, weave or dye yarn in the process of turning raw sheep's wool into serapes, blankets and tapestries.

Archuleta has taught many of her twenty-eight grandchildren—and now even great-granddchildren—to weave. They'll soon be old enough to use their great-grandfather's looms. Most of Eppie Archuleta's dozen-plus looms were hand-built by her weaver husband.

Now in her seventies, Archuleta has gathered many honors during a lifetime of accolades for her skill. Most recently, President Clinton invited Archuleta and her daughter, weaver Norma Medina, to participate in the inauguration ceremonies. They demonstrated spinning and weaving on the Washington Mall.

Archuleta's work already resides in the Smithsonian Institution collection. She has, in addition, received a Governor's Award for Excellence from her adopted home state of Colorado, and she was the first Hispanic woman to receive one of the National Endowment for the Arts National Heritage Fellowship Awards a few years ago.

In the letter bestowing this prestigious award, Eppie Archuleta was congratulated "not only as an artist and educator, but as a remarkable woman who epitomizes the beauty of the human soul."

Her approach is better summed up by what she told the people from the National Geographic who came to take her picture to mark the national honor: "I just can't keep off the loom," she said.

RON KENT

Pine Bowl Maker; Kailua, Hawaii

An unconventional Hawaiian securities specialist has made wooden bowls in his "spare" time for the past twenty-five years. He does neither trading nor woodworking the way other people do, however. He dreamed up a financial seminar called "Practical Finances for Impractical People," and he has advised people on how to invest via a radio talk show.

Still, that's nothing compared to his highly nonconformist bowl-making. In an introduction to the exhibition "Artists of Hawaii," he offered the following: "Without any apologies for the finished product, I can honestly say that my techniques verge on the barbarian."

Kent also claimed in a 1991 interview that his personality changes as he shapes each bowl. To start with, he goes at the raw wood with a vengeance. The final finishing process almost always approaches meditation as he finish-sands his bowls up to fifty times.

The wood he uses comes from the Norfolk pine, a tree imported by mariners to Hawaii from Australia in Captain Cook's day as lumber for spars and masts on sail-powered vessels. The Norfolk pine grows to fifty feet tall and four feet around.

Kent works from leftover chunks whose shape and size decide the bowl's eventual dimensions. He rough-turns log pieces on a lathe, freezing the unfinished bowl (this arrests the growth of a dark fungus that gives the wood its distinctive decorative markings), later soaking

them in a boiled linseed oil solution that completely permeates the wood.

"I leave my work in the oil 'til it is so saturated it no longer floats," says Kent. "Then I dry it, wait a few days and repeat the process.

"After that comes a cycle of soak, rub with very fine waterproof sandpaper immersed in oil, wipe and dry. This cycle is repeated two or three times a week for three to six months, depending upon the individual piece."

It is during the soaking and subsequent rubbing that the true natural beauty of the wood emerges. It is the quality that makes Kent's Norfolk pine bowls especially prized.

"Greys become stark black; ivory takes on various shades of golden yellow," he says. "In some places—unpredictably—the wood shows an amberlike translucence, allowing you to look into or actually through the wood."

EDDIE DOMINGUEZ

Mixed Media Artist; Tucumcari, New Mexico

Eddie Dominguez had a dream. It involved almost one thousand artist's helpers.

The New Mexico mixed media artist believed that the mural commissioned by the city of Tucson, Arizona, for the Martin Luther King Apartments ought to have a community focus and a thematic connection to King's dream of cooperation for the common good.

He enlisted the help of nine hundred-plus Tucson-area residents, nearly seven hundred of them local students, to create and assemble a 1,002-square-foot ceramic tile mosaic mural for the West Facade of the King building on Fifth Avenue in Tucson.

The four-foot square panels ended up being pieced together from thousands upon thousands of donated commercial tiles broken into colorful shards by the students. They form a huge album "quilt" that extends fifty-five feet across the King building, incorporating many hearts and hands—in design and in reality.

"The patches suggest time, work, learning, love and change," says Dominguez, "elements that every human life and society have to deal with individually and collectively."

"The viewer may 'read' the grid in a variety of ways and is challenged to participate in deciphering its symbols," he says. "The irregular bottom edge suggests the possibility of additional 'patches' of a mural in the process of unfolding—a story yet to be completed."

Dominguez's own artistic story has been unfolding since he created his first installation—an elaborate Christmas set—in the sixth grade. The chapters have changed, but his recognizable dinnerware, decorated doors and dressers and mixed media installations have consistently reflected his passion for the southwest and, particularly, for his own home community of Tucumcari, New Mexico.

"I like the idea of 'home'—it's romantic but confrontational," he says. "I grew up in Tucumcari looking at all these strange things that people made—little shrines in front yards,

my grandmother's altar with these spiritual things all arranged with special meaning. I was fascinated by it all."

"The art of the people inspires me and influences me to share this feeling and expression that comes from my heart, my home. My own art is very much a combination of my training in ceramics, my experience, my family and my culture."

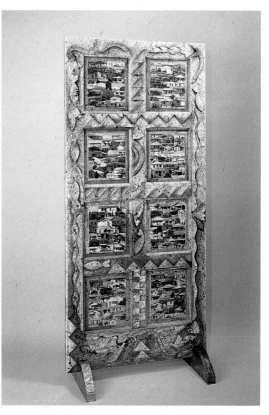

Above: "Neighborhood," mixed media, 83" x 36" x 2".

Left: Installation at the Martin Luther King Apartments, Tucson, Arizona.

STEPHEN KILBORN

Potter; Pilar, New Mexico

On his twenty-fifth birthday, Stephen Kilborn put it all behind him—his former jobs in the mobile home, furniture and ketchup factories, that is—and decided to put his dreams on the line. He would make a living as a full-time potter in Santa Fe, New Mexico.

"The first full year of my new career I worked twelve hours a day, seven days a week and ended up making about $1,500," he says.

Next stop: Pilar, New Mexico.

Kilborn and his wife moved from Santa Fe to Pilar, south of Taos, in 1977, where they had to wait three years for a phone on one of the three eight-party lines.

Over the years Kilborn's "definitely Taos-style" pottery has grown steadily more popular. He now works forty-hour weeks, employs five

people, and sells to shops and galleries around the country. "The amazing thing is that I sell almost half of my work out of the studio here in Pilar," he says. "I think Pilar itself helps to sell the pots.

"Even after seventeen years of living and working, no matter where I travel I still think it is beautiful here on the Rio Grande, and I still feel it's the place for me to work."

ROWDY PATE

Horsehair and Rawhide Braider; Pearsall, Texas

Right now I've started making a banjo for the grandson," says Travis "Rowdy" Pate, Texas rawhide braider.

This banjo—the first Rowdy Pate has ever attempted—has a stretched rawhide drum. It's only meant to be a toy, "but it's starting to sound alright," Pate says, disbelieving.

"I've got a garage full of junk of all kinds," says Pate. At least some of the "junk" is rawhide, whole or cut into strings that will be plaited by Pate into bridles, quirts, lassos and Spanish *reatas*. Pate practices this almost lost art, common in horse country before the advent of nylon rope.

"Primarily I'm a rawhide braider. Some of it is horsehair work and some of it is rawhide," he explains. "I do more rawhide work. I do some horsehair hitching."

Through the Texas Folklife Resources group, he is often invited to display these skills at folk festivals—including at the Smithsonian Institution's Inauguration festivities in Wash-

ington, D.C.

In the old cattle country of South Texas, rawhide and horsehair braiding were skills enjoyed by cowhands in their off-hours. They kept their hands busy while they spun Western yarns.

Rowdy Pate is one of the few Texans who can still do both at the same time. These days he does a lot of boasting about that fine grandson of his. "He's three—he's gonna be a rawhide and horsehair braider," he says.

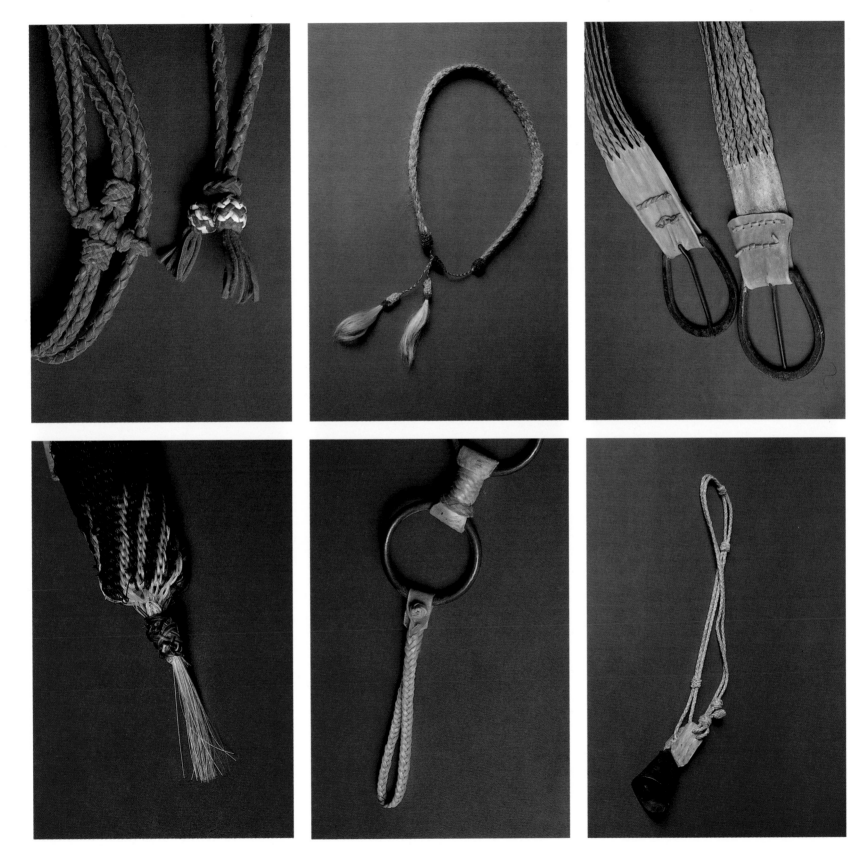

ANDREW GLANTZ

Furniture Maker; Salt Lake City, Utah

Andrew Glantz does most of the work on his furniture by hand, in his creekside studio in Utah's Emigration Canyon. It might take him nine days to make a chair that achieves all the goals he sets for himself—a piece that is attractive, proportional, "sensual"—in summary: "comfortable to the body, and rational to the mind."

An artist in the contemporary crafts tradition who looks to the work of architect/designers Greene and Greene and woodworker Sam Maloof (see page 136) for inspiration, Glantz began as a student in the graphic arts, following in the footsteps of his professional photographer father.

He taught graphic arts until 1978, when he found out he could make more money doing carpentry and odd jobs. His woodworking matured during the three years his family lived on

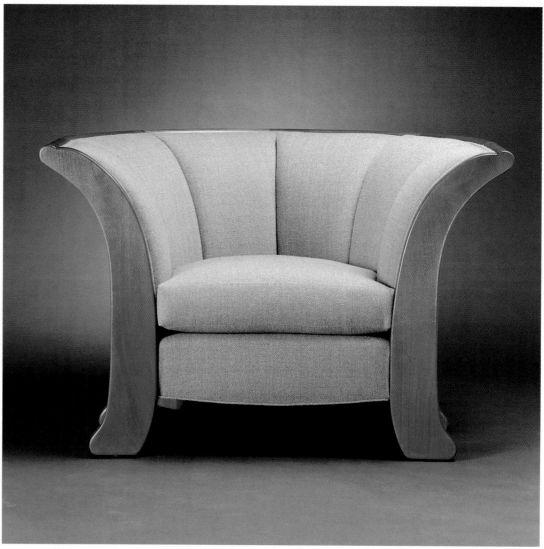

the Navajo Reservation. He followed his doctor-wife's career to Salt Lake in the late 1980s, re-establishing his own furniture firm there, Zenith Design.

To celebrate 1993 as the Year of American Craft, Glantz curated an exhibition of handmade Utah furniture called "Sitting Pretty." His stated goals included providing emerging artists with a chance to show their stuff and allowing the public to sit down on the chairs on display.

Art is about "access and insight" to Andrew Glantz, as well as personal growth.

"This dialogue between what 'I see' and what I'm able to realize [in my work] helps me to continue to challenge myself to push the limits of my abilities," he says.

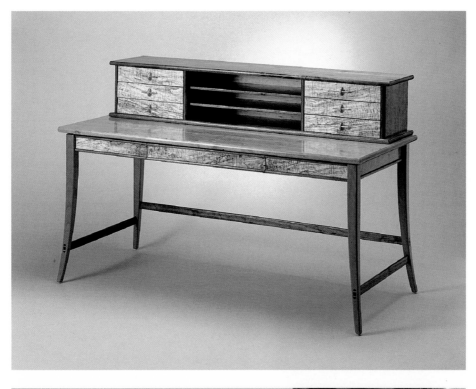

THE MIDWEST

JANE SASSAMAN

Quilt designer; Chicago, Illinois

Jane Sassaman doesn't always call her work quilting.

She might throw in a phrase such as "soft paintings" or "fabric constructions" to describe what she makes. Though they happen to be pieced and sewn of cotton fabrics with cotton batting in between, these contemporary art quilts are meant to be hung on walls, not draped over beds.

Obviously, this Chicago Illinois craftswoman is sensitive to what words might mean and not mean.

"Currently," she writes, "I'm exploring the concept of radiation. 'Radiation' is a word with negative connotations. Coupled with 'nuclear,' it becomes a phrase that terrorizes our world. But I have been considering other meanings of the word. Radiation can be divine or sublime, inspirational or expirational. Consider the radiation of the sun, of the soul, or of the spirit— all emitting from a central source and reaching outward."

Take her work "Information Radiation," which she says refers to the overwhelming abundance of information in our lives. It appears to buzz with radiant energy in zigzag patterns based on the traditional spiral motif.

These symbolize to Sassaman the seasonal cycles of life, as the rays in "Heaven's Gift" signify God-given talent.

Still, Sassaman's pleasure in her work isn't all "heavenly" or spiritual. It's also down-to-earth, primitive and overwhelmingly tactile. "I love fabric," she admits, "the feel, the texture, the colors, the flexibility. I love the craftsmanship quilts demand."

"Summer Garden" (detail).

Quilt artist Jane Sassaman in her studio.

"Night Garden" (detail).

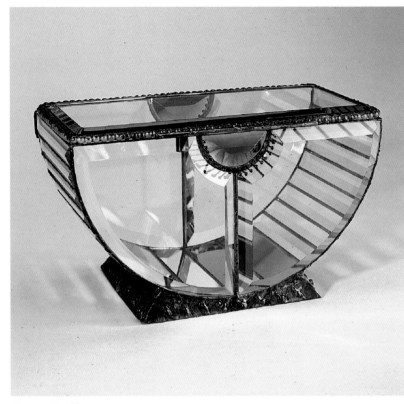

"Dream Box."

"Wish Box."   *Opposite: "Jewel Box."*

ROBERT STEWART

Glass Box Maker; Cary, Illinois

Illinois artist Robert Stewart often mentions children and the child in all of us when he speaks of his efforts to teach himself to cut the beveled glass boxes he's known for far and wide.

There's something childlike—timeless, sparkling and magical—about these jewel-like vessels with their etched and angled facets, which have been hand-ground and polished on antique wheels that the artist preserves for this unique work.

Stewart's boxes exert a universal fascination. One of the first to recognize this quality about them was former Governor James Thompson, who came across Stewart's work through the Illinois Artisans program. Governor Thompson liked to take Stewart's boxes along with him as

gifts when he traveled with international trade delegations.

Now Stewart's one-of-a-kind creations reside in collections of foreign dignitaries around the world.

Russia's Boris Yeltsin and Mikhail Gorbachev each have one. So does China's Deng Xiao Ping and Poland's Lech Walesa. President Bush kept his on display outside the Oval Office.

Stewart believes that children and the most important adults on the planet are exactly the same, in relation to art.

"For a few minutes, when people look at my work, they become children again," he says. "They remember fond memories of the past."

GENEVA BASLER

Quilter, Painter; Anna, Illinois

Geneva Basler's last cow died a summer ago. It had reached the relatively ripe old age of twenty-one, making it three-score years younger than its painter-owner.

Basler was already in her late seventies when she finally gave up milking for mixing colors full-time. Following a lifetime of farming, she planned to spend her retirement years remembering the life she'd always known, chronicling its jobs and joys in painting and quilting.

Basler learned to quilt in the 1920s from her grandmother, back when quilting performed "a social function as well as a practical one."

But it was painting that consumed her thoughts during all the years of hard work, and it is painting that moves her the most. Completely self-taught, Basler paints the things she knows best: field work, horses, cows and the seasons of farming.

A mural depicting Illinois farm life during the Great Depression adorns a state park lodge. And one of her quilted paintings hangs in a new library in the state capital of Springfield.

Now in her eighties, Basler still tends a small garden and lives in her own home, where walls are decorated with murals she has painted. "I feel real good about what I do," she admits. "I had on my mind while I was farming to do this. I knew then that I would one day be painting.

"Some nights when the troubles of the world are on my mind and I can't sleep, I go out on my porch and think about my painting and quilting," she says. "It's a lot better than just sitting wondering what to do with your life."

Basler and her son display one of her heirloom quilts.

MARTIN RATERMANN

Woodworker; Boonville, Missouri

Martin Ratermann, a fourth-generation carpenter, works in a wood shop behind his Boonville, Missouri, home. He cares that his craft, furniture making, has become a part of his family's regular daily routine. "I think it is important for my children," he says, "to understand how I do my work. By fostering their appreciation for the finished product, I teach them why my work means so much to me."

Ratermann claims he receives "a measure of contentment"—personal and spiritual satisfaction—from working with a material of the beauty and diversity of natural wood. He isn't embarrassed to say that his artist's medium humbles him and demands his respect. "As I delve into its mystery, a relationship develops between the tree and me," he says.

A special relationship of another sort happens to be developing between Ratermann and one of the "chips off the old block," so to speak. "Since my eleven-year-old daughter shows a genuine interest in the craft, I see the opportunity to pass my knowledge on to someone else," he says, "who will continue this work in the future."

Above: Furniture maker Martin Ratermann constructs all of his pieces in his own shop by hand. His working technique is in the tradition of older craftsmen, whose hands-on approach to every facet of the craft created unique production work.

Left, a shady garden is the perfect spot for this low-back rocker. Right, this high-back rocking chair resembles the style of master furniture maker Sam Maloof, who continues to be a great influence in Ratermann's work.

The "relationship" between Ratermann and the wood begins early, when raw stock is chosen for his creations.

JAMES T. LAWLESS

Blacksmith, Metalsmith; Nashville, Indiana

James T. Lawless began blacksmithing when his brother, who owns a nursery, asked him to make twenty shepherd's-hook plant stands. In the ten years since, he's made somewhere between forty and fifty thousand more shepherd's hooks to sell—he has lost exact count—and expanded his blacksmithing business to include different traditional items, from wrought-iron boot scrapers to wooden-handled rug beaters to pot racks that incorporate "single trees" from old horse harnesses.

At the Country Anvil, his metalsmithing works in Nashville, Indiana, he hammers out individually handmade items that have been shipped to customers as far away as Japan.

People who ask how Lawless learned to work so familiarly with a medium as unyielding as iron might find out that he once, years ago, welded valves for nuclear power plants and submarines.

His heart, however, belongs to the slow craft of his great-grandfather. "I take time with every piece," he says. "As long as I can hold a hammer, I'll be blacksmithing."

BOB AND CAROL GERDTS

Egg Artists; Greensburg, Indiana

Decorated eggs and egg forms have been visible in the cultures of China, Egypt, England, France and especially Russia, where Carl Faberge, a jeweler, created the world's most famous decorated eggs for the Russian court.

Faberge's eggs were made of ivory, gold, precious metals and gems, styled in an egg shape. But none of the Faberge art was actually made of eggs.

Carol and Bob Gerdts carry on the tradition of egg art, but theirs utilizes real egg shells.

All kinds of egg shells come into play, from small finch eggs for jewelry to huge ostrich eggs for elaborate mantelpieces. The egg seldom used is the chicken egg. "Most of our customers prefer the unusual sizes and types of eggs," Bob says. "The chicken egg is just too common for this type of decorative work."

They decorate their eggs in a variety of ways, from the ornate, intricate Faberge style to their own unique method—"simple but elegant," Bob likes to call it.

Carol was the one originally interested in egg art, and Bob dutifully bought her one per year as a gift. Noting their collecting interest, the artist asked them to attend her egg-art classes, and the rest is craft history. Bob and Carol's Egg-Art has now won awards in five states, and their national clientele continues to grow.

For Bob, whose previous career in data management left him burned out and stressed out, the lifestyle is "egg-xactly" what he wanted.

"I'm my own boss," he says, "but I'm working harder now than I ever did before."

After a moment's thought, he adds with a laugh, "This is a hobby gone haywire."

GLORIA ZMOLEK SMITH

Paper Artist, Quiltmaker; Cedar Rapids, Iowa

Papermaking and quilting each involve bringing small pieces of fiber together to make an artistic whole. This process of integration still excites Gloria Zmolek Smith, now in her tenth year of forming, dyeing, drying and folding handmade paper, from which she constructs nontraditional "quilts." "The individual squares are wrapped like gifts," she says.

Papermaking still seems mysterious and magical to her. "It is a complicated, tedious process, but for some reason unknown to me I derive a great amount of satisfaction from the ritual," she says. She begins with various plant fibers that might come from as far away as the Philippines or Thailand, or from as close as a cattail stand or cornfield out on the outskirts of town.

Whether Smith works with corn, iris leaves, pampas grass or hay, she cooks and beats the fiber for several hours before pigmenting the pulp, molding it and pressing it in a massive paper press in her basement studio, which she calls "the dungeon."

Her subject matter ranges as widely as her materials. "The content of my quilts speak about my children and my concern for the world in which they live," is what she says, but that might mean she's expressing anything from intimate home truths to an international plea for peace.

Her "Calvin," for example, memorialized a family puppy which died (text provided by

"Only a Thousand Lives: Hungary." Handmade paper, kozo, abaca, flax, pigments, foam core. 30" x 33" x 2".

Right: "Only a Thousand Lives: Somalia." Handmade paper, flax, abaca, ferns, wheat, yucca. 9" x 18 x 2".

Smith's nine-year-old daughter Laurel).

Meanwhile, a recent series with a pacifist theme led Smith to assemble forty-three paper quilts—representing the forty-three nations involved in the Persian Gulf War—that incorporate hundreds of paper cranes hand-folded in the traditional Japanese *origami* style.

Smith's flair for integration of separate parts extends beyond her art and into her life, as well. "I have very strong feelings," Smith says, "about being so many people—a wife, a mother, an artist, a cook, a photographer, a framer, a publicist . . . . How to fit all of those things together and remain a sane person puzzles me at times.

"I find much solace in being able to piece together my quilts in a harmonious way."

MAUREEN SEAMONDS

Clay Sculptor; Webster City, Iowa

Maureen Seamonds' workplace is a studio located in the oldest building in Webster City, Iowa—the town's one-hundred-forty-year-old former ice house.

"You can see where the picks were stuck in the wall," notes the artist—exactly the sort of surface detail a fired-clay sculptor like Seamonds would be likely to notice.

Seamonds has exhibited widely in her home state of Iowa, where she teaches and has served, since 1987, as the state's Designer Crafts Association president.

Her large, abstract ceramic works, with their complex layerings of underglaze, stains, paint and metal oxides, provide sensuous, flowing surfaces on shapes that she says are meant to suggest the harmony of the natural world. "The 'earthiness' of clay is downplayed," she explains, "for the full realization of the form."

Some of Seamonds's more recent art, such as "Spirit Gesture," appears as weathered or eroded as an ancient lava flow on a rock face, alluding to the natural process of aging and decline. Other recent work she has etched with a graceful, continuous calligraphic line, as though an unseen hand has written a strange language on stone.

"These forms encourage the incorporation of memory and imagination," she says—in other words, their meaning reveals itself slowly to the eye of appreciative beholders.

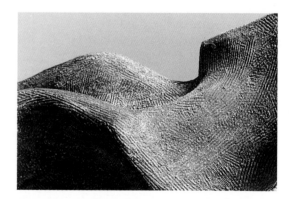

The surfaces of some of Maureen Seamonds's recent works are a complex layering of underglaze, stains, paints and metal oxides. The surface might be covered also with layers of multicolored calligraphic lines.

VERNON BREJCHA

Glass Artist; Lawrence, Kansas

A native Kansan and the son of tenant farmers, prairie glass artist Vernon Brejcha was born in the cow town of Ellsworth and grew up in the tiny farming community of Holyrood—the kind of place, he says, where "fast food" meant "jackrabbit."

As a child he drew incessantly. In fact, it's his earliest memory. Yet he never considered a career in art until he went away to college. At Fort Hays Kansas State, Brejcha saw his first painting on canvas—and took his first shower and placed his first phone call ever. Later, he saw his first artware blown of molten glass and followed its call to his career.

The prairie spirit animates Brejcha's glass always, from his earliest work to this day. He chronicled the trials of the Plains Indians in his Master's show when he earned a postgraduate degree from the University of Wisconsin. Kansas skies reflect in the colors he chose for his "Ominous Cloud Vase" of last year.

His series of blown-glass "dippers," often mistaken for pipes, evolved from the old tin water-dipper that swung from the windmill tower on the family farm.

"I remember that being the coolest and best drink of water in the world," he says, as if the taste still lingers in his memory.

As Brejcha wrote in his introduction to a group show of Plains artists' work, "I want to remain faithful to my prairie roots.

"My memories [of Central Kansas] are what I know best."

"Southwind," blown glass dipper, with "Summer Storm, Post From the Memory Fenceline."

"Ominous Cloud," vase.

"Turbulent Summer, Post From the Memory Fenceline."

JERRY BERTA

Ceramics, Rockford, Michigan

Jerry Berta's ceramics are sheer "diner-might," you might say.

In the old days, Berta's father assembled Chevrolets in a Michigan auto plant, back when cars still had style and fat fins. Sculptor son Jerry started out making miniature ceramic cars.

Today, however, Berta sculpts the roadside attractions of a bygone, car-loving day in pudgy lumps of clay that serve as tributes to a more design-conscious era of Americana.

After he constructs his perfectly appointed mini-diners, he fires them with shiny, iridescent glazes and often lights them with their own miniature neon signs. Then he sells them out of a nontraditional gallery—a restored Flint, Michigan, diner that resembles a gigantic version of one of his sculptures.

His nostalgic imagination doesn't just run to diners. The Berta collection on sale inside the Diner Store in Rockford includes glazed clay movie palaces, burger joints, hot dog stands

The Diner Store—"All art, no food."

Self-portrait.

and ceramic teapots in the shape of kitchen appliances.

The motto of his Diner Store, since he opened in 1988, has been "All art, no food" to keep from confusing tourists driving by. However, since he moved the diner to Rockford and set it up as a gallery, he's bought another prime example of ancient dinerdom and moved it—lock, stock, jukebox and ketchup bottles—from what he calls the "diner capital of the world" (New Jersey).

He set Rosie's Diner up next door.

Now he has the thing he never dreamed of—a restaurant—to serve the patrons of the other, art diner.

Its motto? "Eat and buy art," of course.

KEN PELLAR

Sand-Carved Glass; Detroit, Michigan

The creative spirit lives in all of us, just at different levels," believes Ken Pellar of Michigan.

This spirit sometimes makes itself felt in mysterious ways. That's how it happened in Pellar's case, at least.

"I was introduced to the sandblasting process on glass by a woman who used the technique simply to sign her work," he says. "I immediately began experimenting with more elaborate sandblasting techniques."

One thing led to another as the creative urge

took hold. Floral-patterned etched-glass panels became one-of-a-kind sandblasted tabletops.

"Two years ago, I took my original work in another new direction," Pellar explains. "At present I am continuing to explore new avenues of expression using carved glass in the design of furniture as art."

The artist's custom tables are composed of thick, sand-carved plate-glass tops on bases of metal, wood, marble, laminates and found objects. They've been well received both by gal-

leries and design centers, as well as by private collectors across the country.

His designs draw on his technical art background—Pellar began as a draftsman of patent applications, having majored in mechanical drawing— which is why it seems to have taken him a long time to consider himself a legitimate artist.

"Those of us who are driven by this creative urge often have difficulty recognizing this pursuit as a gift—or a curse," he says. "We are bound by our desire to create."

"Prairie Pow Wow," seven pieces 4' x 8', tabletop 3' x 6'.

MARJORIE AND HAROLD ALEXANDER

Papermakers; Arden Hills, Minnesota

Pioneers in the production of fine paper from renewable resources, Marjorie and Harold Alexander of Minnesota are doing their part to explore ways to protect the earth's diminishing supply of trees.

Paper has been made for over two thousand years, but was not made from wood until 1840. Realizing this, the Alexanders have spent the last seven years studying a variety of indigenous plant and agricultural residue fibers worldwide, seeking alternatives to using wood in the creative art of papermaking.

Marge is a paper artist whose work is exhibited internationally. Harold, known as "Alex" to family and friends, is a designer and associate professor at the University of Minnesota Extension Service. Both enjoy teaching others to make fine, acid-free papers in small community and home settings as a way to generate income in economically depressed areas.

The husband-and-wife team's collaborative efforts have led to their being sent, by the Organization of American States, to Jamaica to establish a hand-papermaking educational center. It is the first such facility in the Caribbean area, converting native Jamaican plant fibers such as banana leaf, bamboo, breadfruit, bagasse (sugar cane) and hibiscus into a variety of fine paper products.

Alex has designed a similar facility in Egypt which they hope will employ up to one hundred and fifty Zabbaleens—the largest community of garbage collectors in Cairo—who collect sixteen hundred tons of waste a day. Marge will teach them how to "recycle" that waste—paper, corn stalk, banana leaves and native pest plants—into fine stationery, note cards, gift boxes and wrappings.

The Alexanders' home state—Minnesota—is also ripe for the picking. Agricultural residues abound in the Upper Midwest. Their home—designed by Alex—sits on moorings above a marsh full of native cattails. Marge harvests their renewable leaves for paper pulp after the wetlands freeze, so that plants and surrounding vegetation are not damaged.

As long as there are new plant fibers to study and people to teach, this environmentally conscious couple will continue to explore alternatives to wood. Newest plans include establishing a hand-papermaking center on a Native American reservation near their home.

Marge explains their mission: "My husband and I are dedicated to sharing our papermaking research and the potential it offers to others both at home and globally. Handcrafting paper from indigenous plant and waste fibers can be a significant catalyst in the movement to combat global environmental degradation."

Opposite: A variety of sample papers made from natural, bleached and colored non-wood plant and agricultural waste fibers.

BERNICE BLAKNEY

Star Quilter, Dressmaker; Santee, Nebraska

Santee Sioux star quilter Bernice Blakney has dedicated the second half of her life to teaching ancient crafts to the younger women on her reservation, hoping to pass the ways of her tribe down to the next generation. "My grandmother raised me and taught me traditional ways until I was sent to the mission schools," she says. "I continued to learn to handsew at those schools, but our Indian ways and language were not accepted. If we talked Indian there, we would be punished."

Blakney currently teaches star quilting, traditional dressmaking and old-time ribbon applique work of the Santee Sioux to her students at Nebraska Indian Community College. She is most famous, however, for her own exquisitely stitched traditional star quilts. Though her ancestors were actually taught to quilt by the missionaries on the reservations, the star has always been an important symbol in Santee traditions and spiritual beliefs.

Star quilts are given to others to commemo-

Santee Sioux quilter Bernice Blakney specializes in star quilts.

rate very special life occasions. It is a great honor to receive one. Star quilts are also given in memory of a deceased loved one at a "give away" ceremony a year after their death.

Only six elderly women on the Santee reservation know how to make a star quilt entirely by hand, and three of them are no longer healthy enough to quilt. Blakney feels it is her special mission to teach younger women of the tribe how to make them.

"The love of quilting is in my blood," she says. "I remember how my grandma would go and quilt whenever she wanted. That's what I do now. For me, quilting is good therapy, and an act of creativity.

"I am very proud of our people and their traditional arts. My hope for the future is that the young women who are quilting now will keep up with it and teach others. It's just so important for our people to keep the traditions alive."

CURTIS AND SUZAN BENZLE

Ceramicists; Columbus, Ohio

Since 1979, Curtis and Suzan Benzle have worked together to explore the artistic possibilities of translucent porcelain. Their vessels are beautifully shaped and designed, but the interplay of light through the delicate surfaces is the process that intrigues both the Benzles and the many avid collectors of their work.

Depending on the color of the vessel's surfaces and inlays, light can make these pieces seem nearly alive, either in a golden, electric glow, or, as Curtis Benzle calls it, a "kinetic presence." Under close scrutiny, this light quality can almost seem like glass. It is most detectable in their larger vessels, but also present in their popular jewelry line.

This innovation adds an element of drama that is unusual in opaque clays, and elevates their work to the level of art.

"Marisa's Song," 8" x 10" x 3".

"Shark's Tooth," 8" x 10" x 3".

"Flying Home".

Right: "Cross Stitch," 4"high x 4"diameter.

VANESSA MORGAN

Garment Maker/beadworker, Anadarko, Oklahoma

Vanessa Paukeigope Morgan is proud to be a Kiowa woman. At age eleven she began learning the traditional female skills of the Kiowa tribe, which include dressmaking, moccasin and legging making, bow-and-arrow making, cradleboard making, saddle making, bowcase/quiver making and more. Her grandmother, wife of the Kiowa Five's Steven Mopope, taught her these things, saying, "Watch me, pay attention, know why you are doing things a certain way. I won't be here

forever!" It is in her honor, and the honor of teachers before her, that Vanessa continues her work, practicing, teaching and communicating the heritage of the Kiowa people. She feels that is her mission now, when so few are carrying on the traditions. "It frightens me," she says, "that our Kiowa cultural heritage, that was once so powerful and beautiful, has almost disappeared. It is more important that I continue my traditional work than to take artistic liberties at this time."

Like her grandmother before her, Vanessa is held in great regard for the quality of her garment and bead work. The National Endowment for the Arts has recognized Vanessa as a Master Traditional Artist, and her work wins awards at art shows for Indians and non-Indians alike.

She makes virtually all the garments, gear and other material customary to the Southern Plains Indians in traditional style, using buckskin, beads, rawhide, earth pigments and a variety of decorative accessories. Her beautifully made garments are seen at Kiowa ceremonials such as the Black Legs Society and O-Ho-Mah Society dances.

While she strives to do fine work at all time, for Vanessa that is of secondary importance. "My work is not an end in itself," she says. "Nor is it something meant to bring me fame or riches. It is simply a perpetuation of the Kiowa people and their culture for the unborn generations after me."

Right: Vanessa Morgan and son Gabe at the Kiowa Black Legs Society dance. Gabe wears traditional society paint, and both wear Kiowa garments made by Vanessa.

Below: At the wedding of Gabe Morgan, both the bride and groom wear traditional Kiowa garments made by Vanessa.

TOM RAUSCHKE AND KAAREN WIKEN

Woodworkers; Palmyra, Wisconsin

Not for nothing did Tom Rauschke and Kaaren Wiken name their home crafts company XN-TRIX. During most of their eighteen-year marriage, they have collaborated on eccentric, intricate creations that combine Rauschke's skill at woodworking with Wiken's passion for embroidery.

Small wonders come to life under their hands—usually miniature natural worlds of birds and wildlife. The couple use the simplest tools for these wood-and-needlework habitats.

In Tom's case, he turns hunks of wood on a 1940s lathe—elm, hickory, oak or black walnut that might otherwise become firewood for their stove—in the process of paring away hardwood to prepare it for carving. "A subtractive process," he calls it.

Kaaren, meanwhile, takes up needle and thread to add her careful contributions. She'll often embroider panels that serve both as an integral part of her husband's creative work in wood and as free-standing decorative pins.

They sound a bit like medieval mystics or forest philosophers when they talk about their happiness with the job they do every day.

"When we begin to work on a piece, the possibilities are infinite, but as we go along in the process, the possibilities become much more limited until, at the end, there is only one choice left.

"To be alive and creative, we try to be aware as we are making each decision of other possibilities and variations, then we do what makes our hearts sing."

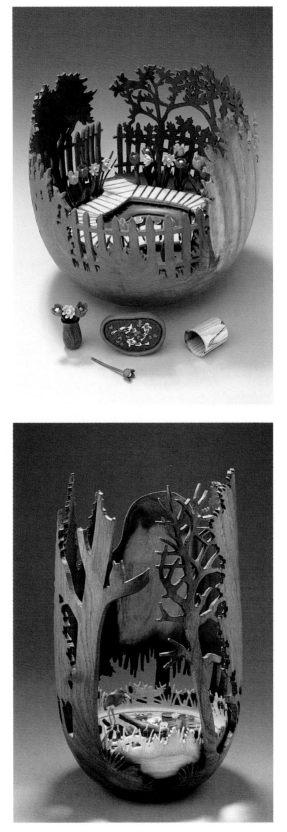

THE NORTHWEST

DOLLY SPENCER

Eskimo Dollmaker; Homer, Alaska

Dolly Spencer dresses her extraordinary Eskimo portrait dolls in tiny mukluks and native-fur parkas, patterned after the clothes she saw her mother make as a child. "I try to do all the work like my mother taught me how to do for ourselves," she says. "Real stuff, native stuff, and that way a person can see how they used to dress."

Her mother's generation never sewed dolls or playthings, says Spencer. "They were always sewing for survival, making mukluks for each family. She never had time to mess with making us a doll." Spencer was, however, able to observe one artisan as a child—the famed Kotzebue dollmaker Ethel Washington.

The youngest of twelve children and the only one born in a hospital, Spencer learned to tan Arctic ground squirrel—an all-day process—at an early age, six or seven years old.

She still tans her own squirrel hides, because tanneries won't do it to suit her, and her own wolverine heads—considered scraps to be discarded by others. Spencer wastes nothing. "The wolverine, you use every bit of that, every bit," she explains, meaning ears, head, belly, paws and tail (she might use wolverine tail hair for her dolls' hair). "That's a wolverine, you don't have no waste."

She spends fifteen to twenty hours, she estimates, carving exquisitely realistic heads for her dolls—which often represent actual people—from rough-hewn chunks of Alaskan birch.

For the authentic clothing, she'll use skin, gut and sinews from many animals: squirrel, caribou, wolf, land otter, bearded seal and, very occasionally, mink ("Mink is no good for nothin' but for looks," Spencer complains). The bottoms of their tiny mukluks are oogruk (bearded seal), shaped by chewing, a process Spencer learned from her mother. Dyes made of alder bark add waterproofing.

All sewing is done with traditional twisted caribou sinew, a process known as skin-sewing.

Arthritis has slowed Spencer down a bit, and good furs have become harder to come by, but the knowledge remains in her hands. Sadly, that's something she's not passing on to the next generation. "Nobody's interested," she says, "not even my daughters."

"I like to skin-sew, you know, what my mother taught me," says Spencer. "I just do it for my pastime."

ANITA DE CASTRO

Ceramic Artist; Ketchum, Idaho

In my ceramics, the challenge is to convey the essence of an idea," explains earthenware artist Anita de Castro, whose goal is to create objects that are simple, beautiful and compelling.

Her fruit-decorated jars and platters and mosaic-tile furniture seem touched with the naiveté of the primitive. De Castro's original painting designs and bright glazes celebrate movement and color.

This former dancer calls red clay "the equiva-lent of the primal urge for me, and I take real pleasure in the richness of color and warmth it so fundamentally gives each piece."

Imagery of the seasons prevails in her mosaic-tile benches and fruit platters.

Perhaps a career in clay was destined for, as a child, de Castro's mother noted, her daughter was always "an avid Jello-patter."

Since those years, her career, like her ceramics, has followed its own intuitive trajectory, taking her from New York City to Idaho's gorgeous Sun Valley. She calls her benches "an invitation to repose in a leafy place," an urge she herself responded to by moving there in 1982.

"My mosaic benches and large, handbuilt fruit pieces speak of the natural botanical world," she says, "reflecting my passion for gardening and country living, for seasons and harvest, for color and voluptuous form.

"There is a singularly direct connection to the piece in handbuilding, for the maker and the recipient, that I enjoy," she continues. "Sometimes I add to that hand-hewn quality by hammering the surface with my hand while the clay is soft."

"Target Platter."

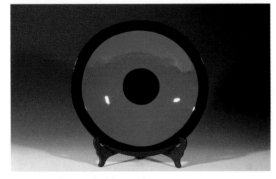

"Black Solid Circle Platter."

"Grape jar."

"Autumn Bench."

DON KING

Furniture Maker; Challis, Idaho

Wherever chair designer Don King goes, he always walks through the woods, stopping to gather any branches and twigs that tweak his fancy.

Nature's wayward humor captivates this artisan, who works the odd quirks of the wood he finds into whimsical, playful shapes.

King earned his bachelor of arts in environmental biology, and first started building rough wood furniture while serving as a range biologist for the U.S. Forest Service.

Typically, as he collects mountain maple, chokecherry, red osier and willow from the banks of the Salmon River near his Idaho home, he might strip some of the wood, dye a few branches, sand one piece and leave the next rough, peeling bark off one branch, but leaving it hanging on another.

Likewise, King's one-of-a-kind chair designs might turn into an upholstered functional form. Then again, it might not. He terms "sculpture" the chairs that no one can sit on.

"I want to work with these woods in a creative and innovative way," he says.

Though well-versed in contemporary architectural and design theory and at home in the abstract, urbane world of art, King confesses, "In my work, there's always an essence of the natural wood that reminds us of the forest environment from which it came."

Above middle: "Chaise Avec Fleur," Maple, willow, elkhide, muslin.

Above right: "Johann's Chair."

"Zebra," maple, willow, elkhide, dye.

"Cascade" coffee table, slate, twig base.

"Kudu."

"Widow's Chair."

DAVID SHANER

Clay Artist; Bigfork, Montana

Nothing in an artist's life is unimportant," clay artist David Shaner says, sincerely. Shaner's studio and home, on the edge of a pine forest near Bigfork, Montana, overlook the magnificent Swan Range. Behind his studio sits a handbuilt, wood-fired kiln. Shaner fired the bricks himself.

Inside the kiln's dual chambers, a down-drawing wood fire exposes the pottery to a swirl of heat that drops a decorative prickling of ash on Shaner's seductive porcelain vessels and brings out dramatic "flashings" in his work.

In addition to firing pots. Shaner builds kilns like the work of art behind his house, a design based on the Japanese climbing-kiln model.

Holder of a master's of fine arts in ceramic design from Alfred University in New York, Shaner has devoted more than thirty years to pottery. He teaches workshops around the country and his has become a name so widely recognized in American ceramics circles that a deep red glaze—Shaner Red—is named for him.

Shaner works and lives as if pottery still has things to teach him, however.

In an autobiographical article, he described his "life's commitment to clay," speaking both humbly and passionately of the happenstance that gives his pottery its sensuous life.

"I enjoy the spontaneity of meeting the pot only halfway," he wrote, "and allowing the process to determine the end result."

Pillow form with mirror openings. 12" x 12" x 6"

A low bowl. 15" x 15" x 7".

Basin with stone, woodfired. 20" x 20" x 4".

A low bowl, triangular construction. 22" x 22" x 3".

DENNIS PARKS

Potter; Tuscarora, Nevada

The story of potter and teacher Dennis Parks involves the story of a town—Tuscarora, Nevada (population sixteen)—where Parks, his wife and their children landed while searching for a new way of life and living. After years of college teaching, Parks bought a hotel in Tuscarora, and started a pottery school. It was destiny for Parks, who has written that "I believed in Tuscarora before I drove up the road." The students came, slowly at first, but now in such numbers that there is a waiting list to get in.

At the Tuscarora Pottery School, pottery students learn from Dennis Parks's technique, to be sure, but also they learn about the potter's life—how to save and share, how to economize where they can, and how to discover what they want to do—not what they *should* do. It is a perfect setting for potters and potters-to-be, in a beautiful place, with time for discovery.

In addition to pursuing his own visual aesthetic in pots, Parks has spent his time at Tuscarora fearlessly challenging pottery dogma by successfully experimenting with single firing and other technical matters that academic potters either ignore or dismiss. It is part of the Parks method to do so, as he encourages "root thinking"—a "methodology that is long on principles, encourages substitution and expects a variety of solutions to flower. This philosophy is nurtured by and finally becomes ingrained in potters on a low budget. You thrive like a weed in any soil, in any climate, in good weather or bad."

Parks's own story has much to do with such thriving, coming as he did from academic security to the unknown wilds of Nevada. But he dismisses the idea that he knew what he was doing. When asked how he came to live in Tuscarora, he says with humility, "I got lost."

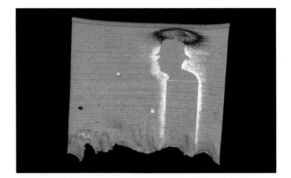

"Self Portrait—Contemplating the Basics."

"Only Because It Was Forbidden."

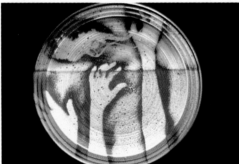

"How They Brought the Good News from Ghent to Aix."

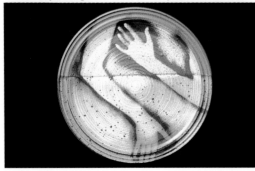

MARY LEE FULKERSON

Narrative Basketmaker; Palomino Valley, Nevada

The family of fourth-generation Nevadan Mary Lee Fulkerson came West even before the Gold Rush of 1849. They made their home among the Paiute and Shoshone Indians in the Great Basin—a vast desert area that stretches over five states and includes Death Valley and the Mojave Desert.

Fulkerson remembers mystical stories her father told her as a child—fairy tales and fables, mysterious legends whispered by Native American elders around a campfire. Those stories, and a fascination with the ancient water jugs woven by the Paiute and Shoshone Indians out of native desert plants, are the inspiration behind Fulkerson's now-famous "story baskets."

"I had been fascinated with an ancient process once used by Paiute peoples living in this arid Great Basin region—they covered their twined willow baskets with pinon pitch; and water, their life's blood, could finally be carried and stored. For them it was a life-giving miracle. For me, watching the paper dry and cling, skin-like, into my basket ribs—it was magic."

Fulkerson's home and studio are in the desert, at the edge of an Indian reservation. Walks through the desert provide Fulkerson with the juniper and willow she needs for her baskets, and with the feathers, bleached bones, pine cones and other treasures she weaves into her baskets for decoration. After she constructs her baskets, she applies paper pulp, then paints colorful stories on the vessels, reminiscent of the ancient legends of those who occupied the Great Basin before her.

Fulkerson's award-winning baskets are exhibited worldwide, but she is perhaps proudest of founding the Great Basin Basketmakers Guild in 1983, which now boasts over 125 members. She is currently writing a book entitled *Peoples of the Sage: Native American Basketmakers of the Great Basin.*

Fulkerson is spiritual about her art. Names of her baskets include "Spiritual Journey," "Spirit Shrine," "Legend of the Stone Mother," and "Thought Woman Creation Myth."

"A basket comes from the earth, transforming into another being," she said in a newspaper interview a few years ago. "They sing and dance around the universe before they die a natural death. Then, they lie in the earth, waiting to be reborn."

"Rainbow Shrine Basket."

"The Grandmother and Her Magic Willow Thread."

SUSAN DAVY

Potter; Burlington, North Dakota

Potter Susan Davy announces, "I'm the only full-time potter in the state, but keep in mind there are only six hundred and fifty thousand people in the whole state of North Dakota!"

"It's a wonderful place to come home to," she says, which is exactly what she did when her grandparents died and she bought the only piece of property she said could bring her back home. Their farm is now home to her very active studio—designed by her architect brother and built by Davy, her husband and father. It was an earth shelter until very recently.

"Hobby building" was her father's forte—boats, chairs, desks, tables. The Davy children always had access to his shop to tinker. The whole family was artistically inclined. "We painted, did all kinds of craft projects and we made beautiful mud pie sculptures when it rained. My mother never cared if we were clean and neat—she was very supportive of our mud pies," Davy remembers.

"I always loved this farm," she says. "My grandfather was a wheat farmer who supplemented his farming habit with a mail carrier's job. He and my grandmother also sold eggs to the local hospital."

Davy is now harvesting a different type of crop on that beautiful farm—pottery…lots of it! She is famous for her signature dinnerware. But, she proudly announces, "After eighteen years, I am finlly getting out of the kitchen!" True to the North Dakota license plate motto— "Discover the Spirit"—she is about to launch a new line of candleholders and other "home accessories" called "Spirit of the High Plains." She is learning how to weld and, in her opinion, her pieces are becoming more "sculptural."

Davy loves her creative life on the high plains. "Pottery is the only thing I have ever done I can get totally immersed in," she says. "Special things happen. I lose all track of time."

SHARON MARCUS

Tapestry Artist; Portland, Oregon

As a graduate student in anthropology, Sharon Marcus felt drawn to the tribal textiles of the people she studies.

Since she abandoned anthropology for art, her creative impulses have refined in the direction of an ancient medieval textile craft—pictorial tapestry.

She has woven tapestry since 1977, but in 1983 she journeyed to study with the masters of this technique in France, where tapestry reached its height in the fourteenth century.

In Sharon Marcus's skilled hands, this age-old art weaves in surprisingly high-tech elements. Sharon generates a blueprint for her finished designs on her home computer screen. She then transfers the lines of light and shadow onto the stretched vertical threads on her loom.

After she has made the initial decisions, she works instinctively, patiently since it might take fifteen hours to weave one square foot of tapestry. In the traditional style, Marcus weaves blind from the back of the loom.

She has lately been intrigued by parallels between archeological excavation and the tapestry weaving process. As an archeologist unearths the past layer by layer, Marcus lays down her ideas one thread at a time.

"I like everything about it," Marcus says of her work, "the research, design and idea development phase, the careful placement of the skeletal warp threads on the loom, selection of the colored fibers to be used in the design and winding of the bobbins, and the wonderfully tactile and exciting process of the actual weaving process."

She hasn't lost her anthropolgist's yen for distant lands and exotic cultures, however. She's an indefatigable traveler, organizing tapestry tours of her own and others' work around the globe, including exchange projects in Costa Rica, Poland and Australia.

"It's important," she believes, "for an artist to be out in the world."

"Journey as Paradigm," 38.5" high x 77 1/4" wide.

"The Persistence of Archetypes" (detail).

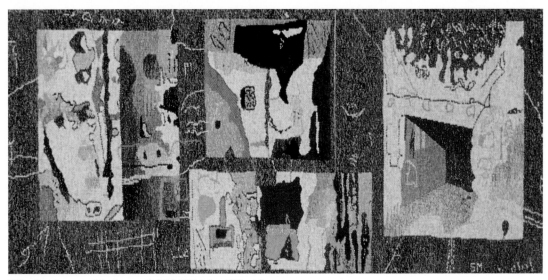

"The Persistence of Archetypes" 37 3/4" high x 75" wide.

ALICE NEW HOLY BLUE LEGS

Porcupine Quill Worker; Oglala, South Dakota

A number of Lakota Sioux families living on the Pine Ridge Indian Reservation in Oglala, South Dakota today are famous for their preservation of traditional Native American art forms.

Four generations of the Lakota New Holy family at Pine Ridge have distinguished themselves as expert porcupine quillworkers. The New Holy family's efforts to revive the almost lost art of quillworking were featured in the film *Lakota Quillwork—Art and Legend*, produced in 1985 by H. Jane Nauman of Custer, South Dakota.

One of the most famous members of the New Holy family was featured in that film—Alice New Holy Blue Legs—who received an award the same year from the National Endowment for the Arts, recognizing her as an Outstanding Folk Artist for preserving and teaching this traditional Lakota craft practiced by no other people in the world.

Alice learned how to quill from her mother and grandmother. "They told me things they were taught by their parents and grandparents," says Alice. There are no books written on these skills. Quillwork was a Native American art form long before European settlers came to America. "It was traditional for the Plains Indians—particularly for the Lakota," according to Alice.

Alice never thought of quillworking as a "lost art" since she grew up in a family of experts. What she later realized, however, was that her family was one of the few families anywhere—on any reservation—still practicing the art.

Hunting the porcupine is in itself a perfected skill. Preparing the dyes and actually dyeing the quills requires a lot of time and patience. The dyed quills are then invisibly sewn to tanned hide with thread. Quills are folded or weaved in ways that create geometric or symbolic shapes and designs, which is where the individual quillworker's true artistry unfolds.

We are, indeed, fortunate that the New Holy Family tradition will continue. Alice and her husband, Emil Blue Legs, have trained their five daughters to quill, and they regularly exhibit their skills and teach workshops to many people who are fascinated with this vanishing Native American craft. Recently the New Holy Family's quillwork was featured in a "Five Families Art Exhibition" organized by Brother C. M. Simon, S. J., Director of The Heritage Center in Pine Ridge.

Alice must feel comfortable with her daughters' carrying on her fine work. In a recent interview she confided she was not doing as much quillworking herself these days. "I think I'm going to get into politics," she said. That is yet another way for her to preserve the great Lakota traditions of her forebears—and to spread their message to the rest of the world.

Quill-wrapping hair ties for a scalp-shirt. In the background are batches of quilts which are dyed and drying.

Right: Quill work in ceremonial attire.

PAUL MARIONI

Artist in Glass; Seattle, Washington

Everyone likes to pigeonhole glass artists, according to Seattle's Paul Marioni. Either an artist should make stained glass or leaded glass or—Marioni's specialty—cast glass. But he ought to do one or another.

To Marioni, who does all three and then some, it doesn't matter. "I use the techniques as my tools," he says simply. "I use the method I need to achieve my vision."

On that day, he happened to be installing a large stained glass work at the University of Washington's eye clinic. A three-panel window on the subject of the eye's capacity, Marioni's work incorporates a new and unexpected material in glass—laminated photographic transparencies.

The connecting thread between this artist's unique and varied creations is his continuing theme—humankind. "My work is generally about human beings, human spirit and human nature," says Marioni, a preoccupation reflected in public commissions such as "The Human Spirit" and "Boxers."

Marioni may be best known, in fact, for these monumental cast-glass works, a technique he and an East Coast artist pioneered in the mid-1970s, developing a similar approach simultaneously.

"It's something that hadn't been done in this country since the late twenties," Marioni ex-

Paul Marioni in the studio with Ann Troutner.

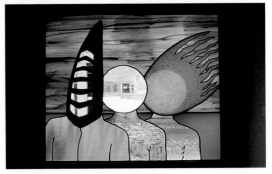

"The Warriors—Shapers of Our Destiny," leaded glass, 36" x 44".

plains. The last great glass-caster was artist Lee Lawrie, who worked during the early Depression years. His cast-Pyrex "Wisdom" was installed in Rockefeller Center in 1933.

Marioni adapted the casting process to sand-casting, a more flexible and less expensive technique than the traditional metal-molding. "We make a pattern of wax and wood, encase it with sand, and pour the glass in," he explains.

It is not, however, molten glass he is seeking to hold fast in his work, but light itself. "I'm working with containing light in certain shapes," he says. "And my work is getting more painterly. More of them are three-dimensional shapes that are painted."

Obviously, it's not going to be any easier to pigeonhole Paul Marioni in the future than it has been thus far.

"Blue House/Yellow House," 21".

JOHN C. MARSHALL

Silversmith; Seattle, Washington

John Marshall's silversmithing extends the reach of what craftsmen have traditionally held possible.

Marshall's free-form designs walk a line between utility and pure, fluid inspiration. From tea services to large, sculptural landscapes in silver, his leaps of imagination blur the distance between the functional and fine art in metal.

His work appears in America's major museums as well as in private, commissioned collections.

The contrasts in his style are distinct.

Square-footed vases or spherical bowls flare wide, as if holding themselves open to the light. One liquid-lit chalice rests on elemental crystals of pale quartz and dark hematite. A pair of candlesticks, serene in their symmetry, dance on flared half-skirts of sterling.

"Function," Marshall wrote in the introduction to a retrospective mounted two years ago at the University of Washington, Seattle, "is an integral part of each piece I do—all parts must work within the design and not in conflict with the sculptural movement."

A professor at the University of Washington since the early 1970s, Marshall devotes himself to bringing along the next generation of metal devotees, artisans' building skills and confidence in a difficult medium.

"I find myself working more conceptually now in my pieces," Marshall explains, "less involved with the craft, confident that my hands will perform as a craftsman."

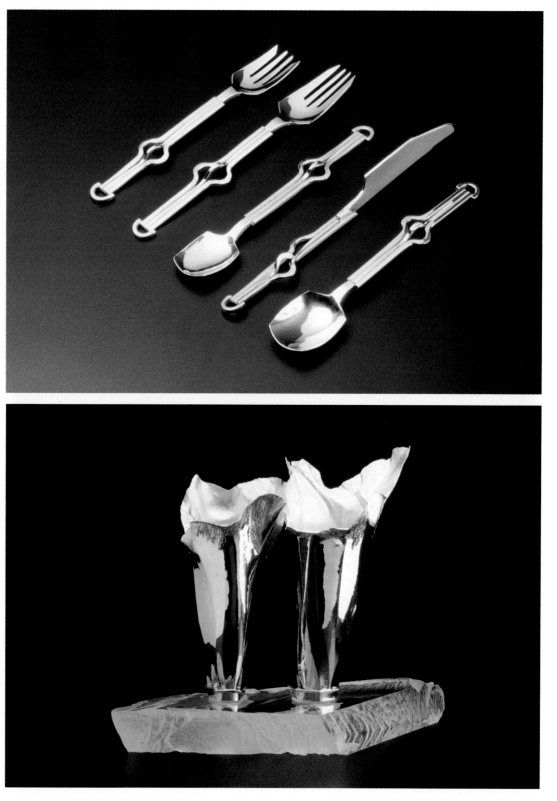

VERLANE DESGRANGE

Saddlemaker; Cody, Wyoming

When other little girls were sewing Barbie doll clothes, Verlane Desgrange was making tack for her model horses.

The daughter of a seamstress and an engineer, Desgrange showed the signs of a precocious craftswoman. She began leatherworking and collecting the tools of her trade at age eleven. By age twenty-four she had found her vocation as a maker of equestrian equipment. With a design degree from Florida State University, the young woman went West to seek her fortune.

She sought out experts in the saddlemaking field, and apprenticed herself first to a maker of Western saddles in Ralston, Wyoming; then to a master English saddlemaker in Portland, Oregon.

The English saddle, she explains, is the more tailored and subtle of the two, its design not having changed much in two hundred years. The Western saddle is more ornate, with fancy tooling and even silver added for flash.

These days Desgrange also teaches saddlery to others. Her stock in trade is fashioning custom saddles to fit both horse and rider (both must be comfortable to enjoy the ride), with the gender of the rider an important consideration in a saddle's construction.

Desgrange considers saddlemaking an undervalued art form that combines engineering, functionality and knowledge of the history of saddlemaking.

"Properly handmade items will wear and wear and wear," says this artist, who still uses pieces of equipment she made seventeen years ago. Since then, she has had to do no more than clean and oil these pieces of equipment.

If there is a secret to quality craftsmanship in this field, Desgrange will know it, and she says: "Just let the tools do the work."

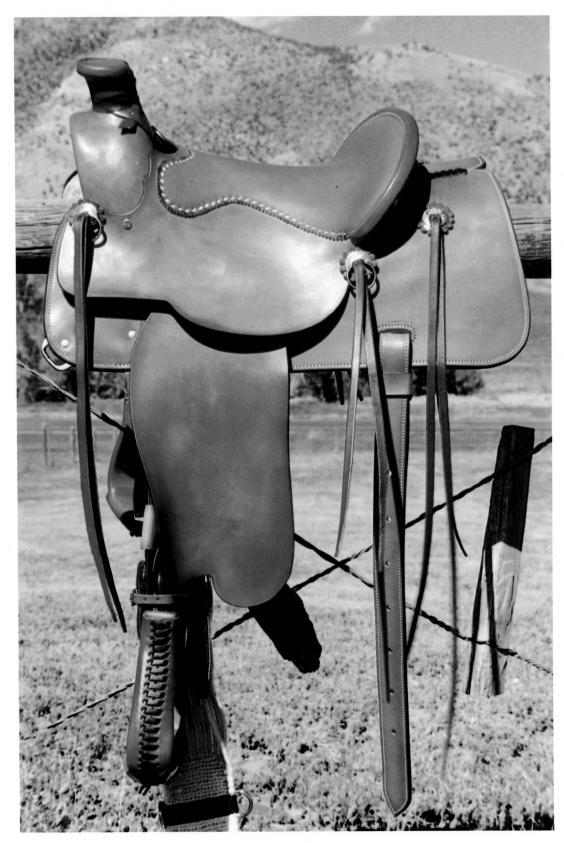

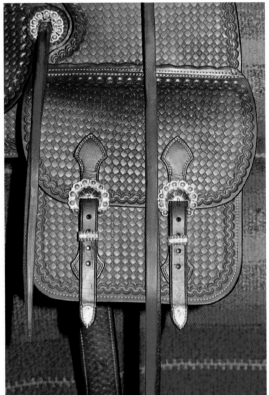

Page 212: Man's "Buckaroo" saddle, stained dark, rough out leather, sterling silver trim.

Left: Plain ranch saddle with overlaid padded seat laced down with rawhide.

Above: Detail of saddlebag buckles and stamping on a ladies' riding saddle.

Right, above: Bridle for man's ranch saddle.

Right, below: Note pad cover; figure carved in color with silver corner plates with gold scrolling by Roy Stokes.

Far right: Texas Trail saddle; historical interpretation of 1890 half-seat Texas trail saddle design; with built-in saddle bags, tapaderos and 9" diameter horn cap.

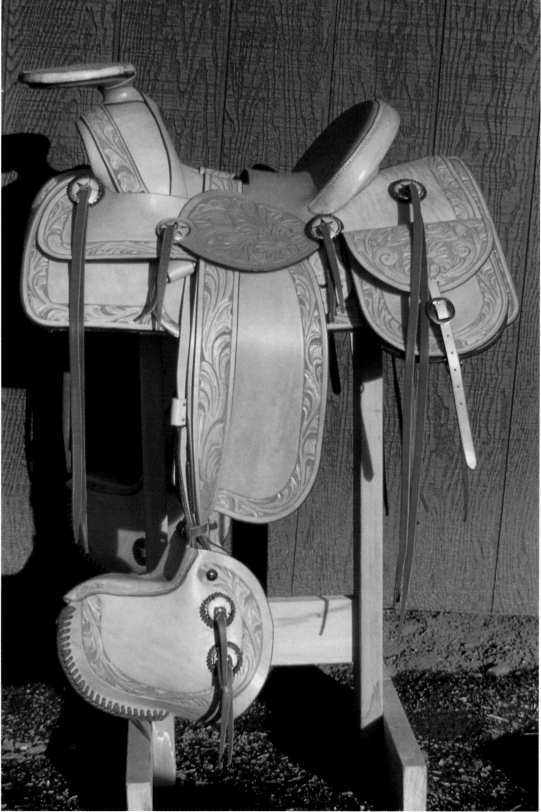

THE PHOTOGRAPHERS